Spiritual Respiration:
I can breathe again

Second Wind

TIFFANY N. SMITH

Disclaimer:
The information in this book is true and complete to the best of the author's knowledge. This story is a truthful recollection of actual events in the author's life. The events, places, and conversations in this book have been recreated from memory.

Hardcover: 978-1-7375440-2-9
Paperback: 978-1-7375440-1-2
Audiobook: 978-1-7375440-3-6
Ebook: 978-1-7375440-0-5

First paperback edition July 2021

Edited by Pam Greer
Proofread by Callie at Proof Corrections by Callie
Cover art by Vanessa Mendozzi
Layout by Sheenah Freitas of Paper Crane Books

Printed in the USA.

This part of the book would normally be the perfect place to publicize one of my many loving family members and speak on how supportive they have been through this entire writing process, but instead I am dedicating this book to any and every person who has ever been in a dark place in their life and felt like they weren't going to ever make it out.

table of
Contents

For I know the thoughts that I think toward you, saith the Lord, thoughts of peace, and not of evil, to give you an expected end.

Jeremiah 29:11

Foreword

I had the pleasure of meeting Ms. Smith my eighth-grade school year in 2018 at Central Middle School. I remember getting my schedule over the summer. The schedule informed me which team I would be on as well as which teachers I would have for the school year. A few of my friends had been placed on the team called "8 White A," which was an Honors Algebra 1 team. I opened my letter and was greatly disappointed to see "8 White B" in bold letters. This team was on the opposite hallway of the 8 White A team. I was frustrated, and complained to my parents that there had to be a mistake because I was supposed to be in an Honors Algebra 1 class. Little did I know, God saw the big picture and had a divine plan for me.

Later, after a phone call to the school, my parents and I learned that Ms. Smith was the math teacher for 8 White B's team, and it was also an Honors Algebra 1 class. As a bonus, my mom knew Ms. Smith from a few interactions at the local community college where Ms. Smith had taken a class. I did some research on Ms. Smith. Many reviews indicated that Ms. Smith was a wonderful teacher. The 2018–2019 school year turned out to be an amazing year. I am one of thirty-one students from the honors class that Ms. Smith speaks about in the book. That year, I felt like I learned more than I had ever learned in math in all of the previous years. I believe this was due to Ms. Smith's love for her students, her different approach to math, and her ability to push us beyond our limits.

After reading the book, I recognized how God had orchestrated everything to line up in her life according to God's will. God's timing is perfect. God is strategic and knows what we need individually to fulfill our purpose. However, we must be obedient. Obedience is key in ensuring that God's will comes to pass. Throughout the book you'll see how obedience is a crucial role in any Believer's walk with God. He has everything planned and laid out for us. We just have to be willing to have faith and trust him throughout the process. Life isn't easy for anyone of any age. In this book, going through the journey of Ms. Smith's life of faith, we can witness how to live life intentionally, how to fulfill God's purpose for our life, and be reminded that God is faithful.

—Sanaa McCloud, Class of 2023

My Promise

My name is Tiffany N. Smith. I am a first-time writer, and if you are reading this book, I am now an author. I know you are probably thinking, Who starts a book off like that? That's easy to answer: me. I could be a bit more formal and act like I am in a job interview. I could give you all the reasons why I am the woman for the job. I know you are thinking, What job? Well, I am the perfect candidate for this job. My job as an author is not just to persuade you to read my book, but to ensure that I deliver on my promise through my story.

Now, I could discuss with you all my remarkable qualities to urge you to read the book. I could give you a list of my strengths and even identify a weakness, which always seems to be a classic interview question, but I believe it will be more meaningful and interesting if those things are revealed as you read the book. I could make an ultimate promise on how your life will forever be changed if you read my book. That's a big promise to make and an even bigger one to keep. Therefore, that is not my promise.

I do promise that *anyone* who reads my story and genuinely digests what is written, no matter the stage of life they are in, will have a deeper appreciation for life, will be provoked to look at life in a different way, and will be inspired to do more and be more and develop hope despite what trials and tribulations they are facing this very moment in life. However, I can only make and deliver these promises by offering you God. God is honestly the center of it all.

WHO *is this book for?*

When I started writing my story—I have to be completely transparent—I didn't know who I was writing it for other than myself. Ultimately, I wanted to write the book for me. It was a personal goal I had put on my list to do about three years ago. However, I also knew, without a doubt, that my story needed to be heard by others. So when I began putting words down on paper, one thing initially became evident: this story is definitely for the Believers—those who believe Jesus Christ to be their personal savior. But as I continued writing, I realized the book is also for those who aren't saved or don't claim Jesus Christ as their personal savior. This book is also for those who are encountering a battle on what to believe or who to believe in and/or those who have decided they don't believe at all. I know you are thinking, How could you possibly write a book for both Believers and nonbelievers alike? Well, I will tell you how. What became most apparent when I finished writing was that this book could help anyone who has experienced anything difficult in their life and felt like they weren't going to make it out. Unless you have lived your entire life under a rock, anyone and everyone in this life has encountered trials, tribulations, and/or afflictions.

The PURPOSE *or why:*

My *why* or the purpose I wrote this book is crucial, but difficult to answer. There are so many reasons people feel they need to tell their story. I ultimately wrote this story to tell both Believers and nonbelievers that God is true to His word, and because of that, you can get through anything and everything you encounter in life with God. Matthew 19:26 says, "But Jesus beheld them, and said unto them, With men this is impossible; but with God all things are possible."

Introduction

Life is too fragile and too valuable to live any other way than intentionally. This should be a Believer's declaration for life. However, those who may not have a relationship with God might disagree. Some would argue, saying, "Life is too short not to follow your heart," or "Life is too short not to live care-free," or "Life is too short, live your best life." At one time there was a trending acronym, YOLO, which stood for "you only live once." It was usually expressed after doing something risky or dangerous.

Though each saying above can be interpreted differently, all promote the same idea: you should do everything and anything you are big enough and bad enough to do in your life while you can because you only get one life, and you never know when your time will be up. Unfortunately, as a Believer, that's not how we should be looking at our life and, even more so, living our life. It's actually quite the opposite. Life is definitely delicate, and having only one life puts so many things in perspective; life is meant to be lived purposefully. God created you for His own purpose. So often, we as Believers miss that important and crucial detail in our life. You weren't created in this life to tell God how you want things to go. Again, that concept is contradictory and constructed by worldly standards. The Bible instructs us to live a life that is holy. God requires a standard. In order for you to live a life that focuses on God's assignment or purpose for your life, you must petition God and ask Him what He wants you to say and what He wants you to do. So many of us Believers fail to acknowledge that God has a perfect will (or plan) for our life. We also fail to acknowledge that God's plan is better than anything we could ever construct. Every day my prayer is "God, let your will be my will for my life. God, please make me aware of your plan for my life and help me to accept it. God, open my eyes and ears so that I recognize the signs and your voice to guide me every step of the way. God, tell me what to say and when to say it, what to do and when to do it, and how to do it according to your will." Any request or petition to God other than asking Him to be head of your life is pointless.

And that brings me to the notions, messages, and/or themes you could extract from my story. If you don't truly consider yourself "religious" or don't believe in the true living God, you may believe that this story is some testament to how great, or what a wonderful person, I am. This story is no testament to a person; this story is a testament to who God is and who He can be, if you allow Him to be head of your life. But let me be clear. I hope to convey one prominent message throughout the entire book and that is: God is faithful. At times, we as Believers don't have a complete understanding of what that truly means. So let me put those words in context.

Yes, God is faithful, but let's examine the depth of that statement. I can best explain it by using God's Word, the Holy Scriptures, which is what we should use as a measuring stick to ensure that what we are saying and doing lines up with God's standard. The Bible should always be the standard. Deuteronomy 7:9 says, "Know therefore that the Lord thy God, he is God, the faithful God, which keepeth covenant and mercy with them that love him and keep his commandments to a thousand generations." Let me give you a quick background just in case you aren't familiar with the Scripture. God had a nation, or people, he initially chose, who are later identified in the Bible as Jews. He didn't choose them because they were some highly esteemed people or because of anything they did. They were actually known for quite the opposite. The Bible calls them disobedient, stubborn, and unbelieving. So what would cause God to remain faithful to such people? We as Believers often fail to understand that God isn't faithful to a certain people, but God is faithful to His word. If God makes a promise, He keeps it. The book of Numbers chapter 23 verse 19 tells us, "God is not a man, that he should lie." Therefore, we must accept both sides of that sword. Yes, God stays true to His word, but that includes God's love as well as God's correction. All through the Scriptures, God speaks about His promises and His blessings, but He also speaks about the correction and judgment He renders when we fail to be obedient. Since God honors covenant and what He says in His Word, He will do exactly what He says He's going to do if it's to encourage, uplift, hold accountable, judge, or chastise. God promises to be faithful to it all. This is why this book is truly for anyone and everyone who reads it, Believer and nonbeliever alike. God is who He is, despite who we decide to be or not to be. Through my story, what I hope I have made most clear is that God is faithful to His word, and if we are obedient to that same word, God is ultimately faithful to us.

chapter 1

Who Is This Tiffany?

*T*iffany & Co., one of the most expensive and famous jewelry stores located in New York, was where my mom got my name. She told the story anytime we were at a family function with my aunts and Aunt Helen was mentioned. My great-aunt Helen lived in New York, and when my mom was young, she went to visit her and rode past the Tiffany & Co. jewelry store. As soon as my mom saw the name, she loved it. "When I have my first daughter, I am going to name her Tiffany." She stayed true to her word. Tiffany Nicole Smith is a very common name. I have met quite a few Tiffanys in my life, even a few with my first, middle, and last name. However, no one is quite like me.

I am the oldest sibling of three. Being the oldest means you have to be the responsible one whether you like it or not. You are considered the second mom even if you don't desire to be. I can remember at around the age of eleven, my mom told me she was pulling all of us out of after-school care because they couldn't afford it. She instructed me that I would need to keep an eye on my brother and sister after school until she or my father got home from work. She usually got home before my dad since he taught in Galena, Maryland, which was about thirty-five minutes from the house. My mom worked at a call center in Dover, which was only about five minutes from home. She kept a list of emergency numbers as well as the number of every family member and friend we knew handwritten next to the phone. "Don't call the job unless it's an emergency! Don't answer the door for anyone. If you are hungry, get a snack out of the cupboard. You can use the microwave, but don't touch the stove. And no one is allowed outside until I or your father gets home!" These were the cardinal rules for being home after school by ourselves.

Anytime either of my siblings broke one of the rules, I would immediately call my mom's job to tell on them. It's funny how as soon as I picked up the phone, I knew it was the wrong move. Yet I was determined to get my brother or sister in trouble, so at the time, it seemed worth it. It had become a routine. My mom would come home and say, "Don't call my job unless it's an emergency, Tiffany. You can't keep calling my job every time you get into an argument with Resa or Kevin. Resa and Kevin, you need to listen to your sister when we are not home. She's in charge." Then the minute they didn't listen, I would call her job.

My mom was the glue in our home. She kept everything together. "Terry with a y," you would hear her say whenever she spelled her name. My mom had a hyphenated last name, Pauls-Smith. "Honey, I am a Pauls!" She expressed confidence when reassuring others, and she had no problem getting things done because of her strong family upbringing. She was a hard worker, determined, and loving. She was very proud of who she was and where she came from; she was born and raised in the Eastern Shore of Maryland.

Growing up, we spent many weekends in Maryland visiting my mom's family. Her family was very close-knit. My mom, brother, sister, and I would often go to Maryland on Saturdays to my aunt Donnie's house for dinner, events at church, or just to visit. Aunt Donnie, whom most of the family called "Nana," was the matriarch of the family. She hosted most of the family functions along with my uncle Jackie, who lived directly across the street from her. My mom was the youngest of seven siblings; therefore, we had a host of first cousins. We spent so much time together, our dynamics were more like brothers and sisters. Many of my childhood memories include watching my mom and her sisters and brothers trying to get live crabs out of the barrel and into this huge silver pot to steam them. It was always entertaining to watch as a kid because my uncle Larry, the youngest brother, was the crab catcher and cooker. Every time he cooked crabs, he would always have one crab he couldn't seem to get out of the barrel and into the pot because it was latching on to the clamps for dear life. Anytime we went to Maryland to see my mom's family, it was a guaranteed good time.

My dad didn't always come with us when we took our frequent trips to see my mom's family. My dad was more of a homebody and introvert, which was funny in itself since he was a middle school teacher. One of the tasks he gave me and my brother when we were older and my dad was nearing the end of his career was grading his papers. He had glaucoma, a blinding disease, which made it difficult for him to read and grade papers. He would give us a key, grade the first paper in the pile as an example, and give us a stack to grade. My dad taught a few subjects over his thirty years of teaching, but for the majority of his time as an educator, he taught English language arts (ELA). This meant we helped grade long essay-like papers most of the time; it seemed to take forever just to grade one paper. Though my dad taught in Maryland, we lived in Delaware where he was born and raised; he had grown up in a small rural town called Townsend. My parents met at a baseball game. At the time, my dad played in an adult baseball league in Maryland called Eastern Shore. My siblings and I often heard about my dad's baseball career "that could have been" but didn't happen because, right at the height of his baseball career, he had begun to lose his sight. His loss of sight affected so much of his life, including having to retire from teaching earlier than he desired. It also caused him to lose his driver's license. My brother and I became our dad's transportation near the end of the year he officially retired from teaching. My dad was what many would consider old-fashioned or traditional. He was the "man of the house." He paid the bills, he was the final authority in the home, and he was a man after God's own heart. He took all of his roles very seriously; he took his role as a God-fearing man more seriously. There were things that just weren't going to happen in his house. "Daddy's here, turn the music off!" you could hear any one of us belt out after school as my dad was pulling into the driveway. We weren't supposed to listen to rap music. Music with cursing had better not be heard from anyone's room. He battled my mom about anything that didn't honor God. Halloween, school dances, makeup, and inappropriate movies were all a no in the home. My dad had a standard. My mom was the parent you went to first to ask for permission for things that were in a gray area. She would sometimes say yes, but most of the time the response was "Ask your father," which usually meant the answer was going to be no. I remember thinking around my teenage years, *I can't wait until I grow up.*

The funny part was that we, as a family, didn't consistently go to church when we were young. My dad went to his church faithfully every Sunday by himself. My mom took me, my brother, and my sister to her church mostly during holidays or if some event was going on at her church. This was because there was a battle about doctrine, or what they believed to be God's standard, in our house. My parents were both Christians, but my dad seemed to adhere to a stricter version of guidelines. My mom had grown up going to a Methodist church. My dad had grown up going to an Apostolic church. The "who is right" battle appeared to be never-ending in the house as I was growing up.

Despite the differences, they both displayed Christian principles in their actions. One thing about my mom was that you could always find her in a posture of prayer and always reading her Bible. She would frequently call out, "Can someone bring me my Bible?" which was usually in the bathroom on the back of the toilet. Weird place, but most of the time, that's where she could get peace and quiet to read God's Word. At the kitchen table, you wouldn't dare put a morsel of food in your mouth without saying grace. And anytime someone was confirming my mother's attendance at an event, she would preface it with "God willing." Though my dad was the preacher in the family, my mom was the one who consistently taught and encouraged Christian practices in our home. My dad didn't remind us to say our prayers at night or get on us about saying grace before we ate, but he taught us through how he lived: he practiced what he preached.

However, despite the battles that took place in our home, my parents were both godsent. Their differences in parenting styles, who they were, and where they came from actually complemented each other; having both of them gave me and my siblings a decent balance. My parents were and still are a true blessing. We grew up in a two-parent household that put God first. We didn't have to worry about alcohol, drugs, or any kind of abuse or neglect in our home. I watched my parents work hard to give all three of us everything we needed and a lot of what we wanted. I don't mean just material things: they gave us love and instilled morals, values, and a strong belief system in our lives. Anyone who knew our family would say the same, especially all the children who lived on Hampton Drive, the street where I grew up. We were "that house" in our neighborhood: the house where everyone came to hang out, the house where you'd get snacks and ice cream, the house where everyone went to play a good game of basketball.

My father bought my brother a portable basketball court for him to improve his basketball skills with. This court attracted all kinds of ball players, girls and boys, Black and white, from any neighborhood that was in close proximity. On any day after school, you could see anywhere from five to forty kids, ages nine and ten years old to eighteen years old, hanging out, playing five vs. five pickup games, on the side-lines waiting for their turn to play, or cheering on the players already in the game. Despite how many kids were out there, or their ages, there was never any drama on the court. The only drama that ever surfaced was my brother getting mad about my sister wanting to play basketball with the boys. Everyone who came to our house to play on the basketball court was aware of my father's standard and beliefs and appreciated my mom's welcoming and loving personality;

everyone respected my parents, from the youngest to the oldest kid. Great memories were made on Hampton Drive.

Though the memories made on Hampton Drive were by far some of my favorites, the memories that stand out the most are definitely of my high school years. I remember sitting in a school-level discipline hearing my freshman year at Dover High School by way of my ninth-grade English teacher, Mr. Andres. English language arts was never a strong suit of mine. I was more of a math person. To me, ELA was boring. I guess I wanted to spice class up by being obnoxious. The problem was, I was more than obnoxious—I was flat-out rude. I had been somewhat mouthy in middle school, but high school had created a whole new monster.

I cannot honestly say I know why I started acting defiantly, but I can tell you it started in high school. I guess Mr. Andres was the first victim. Anytime he spoke in class, I had a rebuttal. Mr. Andres put me out of ELA at least once a week for "running my mouth." This went on for weeks, until he finally got sick of me. About midway through first marking period, he decided he'd had enough. He wrote up a school discipline referral for me for the last time. A discipline referral is a process teachers take when a student's behavior is disrespectful, destructive, or interrupts the learning environment. It's a way to tell the administration that more intense support or severe actions are needed in addressing an ongoing disruptive behavior with the specified student. After the student has received a specific number of referrals for the same behavior, they are sent to a school-level discipline hearing, which includes the student, a parent or guardian, a team of school administrators, behavior staff, and any other appropriate staff, to decide next steps. My dad came to the hearing. I sat in this school-level hearing realizing I might finally come face-to-face with my fate for constantly "running my mouth." My mom always thought it was best for Dad to handle the discipline issues since he was an educator himself. My mom also had an outspoken personality, like me, which didn't always help in these types of settings. I can remember chewing gum as the administrators, Mr. Andres, and others I didn't know began discussing options and next steps.

"Spit out that gum right now!" belted out my dad. Despite his reserved demeanor, he did not tolerate disrespect of any kind from his children. The associate principal at the time passed the trash can in my direction so I could spit out the gum, as he had no doubt in his mind by my father's tone that I was going to comply.

Mr. Andres explained that he would no longer tolerate my disrespect and refused to allow me back in his classroom, as I was a "constant disruption to the educational process." The administrators advised me that being kicked out of ELA at this point in the school year would guarantee that I would fail ELA. This would also keep me in the ninth grade since whatever grade level ELA class you were scheduled in determined your grade level. I remember thinking how embarrassed I would be if I had to repeat ninth-grade ELA the following school year as technically a sophomore. I immediately began begging Mr. Andres for another chance. I promised him that he wouldn't have any more issues from me. My dad sat quietly. I recognized what my dad was doing. He was letting me face my own fate. He was going to be present in these meetings because he was a great father, but he was also going to let accountability have its way because he was fair and believed wholeheartedly in accountability; he realized some things I was going to have to learn the hard way. I kept my promise to Mr. Andres. I didn't cause Mr. Andres any more anguish for the rest of the school year. However, that promise was only for his class and expired immediately upon completion of ninth-grade ELA. Unfortunately, that same rebellious spirit followed me for the remainder of my high school life.

I was a mouthy, defiant teenager who had a rebuttal for anyone in authority. If you said left, I would say right. If you told me to sit down, I would stand up. If you told me to talk, I wouldn't say a word. I had a true case of oppositional defiant behavior, but the majority of the time it only took place at school. My parents wouldn't put up with a bit of disrespect from me or my siblings at home.

It added insult to injury during these school conferences when they found out my father was an educator and a God-fearing man. The teacher, school officials, or principals involved in the incidents seemed surprised when my parents walked in. My parents were both poised and professional. My mom usually held an administrative job and always dressed to impress when she stepped out of the house. Because my dad was a preacher of the Gospel as well as a successful middle school teacher and well respected in the community, he rarely went anywhere without having on a suit. Immediately, I could tell the teachers couldn't make sense of it. When they saw my parents and me all together at these meetings, their facial expressions said, "This doesn't add up." Even now in education, when a child is defiant, teachers often think that the parents are to blame.

Now, what made my mom very different from my father was her assertiveness and outgoing personality. She didn't take any "stuff" from anyone. She could at times be mistaken as aggressive. She had no problem speaking up about anything that needed to be said in any forum. My dad was more reserved, never controlled by emotion, but was instead logical. He observed, listened, and took mental notes before he spoke a word. In his book, life was simple. Life was black and white. Right was right and wrong was wrong. He would immediately set me straight in the presence of other educators, but not like you would expect him to since he worked in education as well. He was a listener, and he made sure to advocate for me when he believed I was right. I'm not sure if my parents somehow knew that the fire that was in me would one day be used for good, but they kept me in line. In a way, my parents accepted my outspoken demeanor, always careful not to break my spirit or change who I was. My parents used my high school years to mold the bold spirit in me instead of trying to destroy it. Either way, I never let my behavior impede my grades.

Because my grades were good, I only applied to two colleges. Both colleges were in Maryland, which seemed convenient since my mom's family lived there. I felt like I needed to get away from home, but not too far. I thought it was the perfect plan. Unfortunately, it wasn't God's plan. I didn't get accepted to either of the two colleges.

"God has a plan," my mom uttered to me as I read aloud the second denial letter I had received. "Let's just go up to Delaware State University's admissions office and talk to someone." Delaware State University (DSU), a Historically Black College and University (HBCU), was the local college. I hadn't even thought of going there simply because I thought I wanted to go out of state. However, at this point, I didn't have any options as far as colleges go, so I needed to make some decisions quickly. I remember walking into the admissions office with only an official high school transcript in my hand to speak to the head of admissions. After a very informal but productive meeting with my mom, the head of admissions, and myself, I walked out of the office with two scholarships, one for academics and the other for my SAT scores. Needless to say, I officially became a Delaware State University Hornet.

I majored in sociology with a concentration in criminal justice at DSU. It only made sense since my lifelong dream was to become a lawyer. As early as elementary school, I had been selling my dream to my parents about becoming a lawyer. I completely believed that the bold streak in my life was a surefire sign that I would someday stand up in a courtroom and argue. However, the goal was far from my mind when I began freshman year; during my first year in college I was consumed with partying. I was unofficially the "tequila queen" among my intimate group of freshman friends. I spent most of my time with friends I had known locally, and I met a few new friends at DSU. We partied at least two nights a week plus the weekend. I prided myself on the ability to take down almost twelve shots of tequila before passing out.

Being a commuter was perfect for me. I would arrive on campus to hang out and go to events, then go to dorms and apartments for the after-party events, but go home to sleep in my own bed. I had this false sense of security with regard to my studies that I had gained while in high school. High school had taught me I could keep good grades while exhibiting so many immature behaviors. I was reminded real quick that this unfruitful behavior had cost me something in high school and was also going to cost me something my freshman year of college. I'm not sure why I hadn't learned my lesson in high school. Maybe because, previously, this unruly behavior had only cost me time out of school and conferences with my parents and/or teachers writing me discipline referrals. Never had my unruly behavior cost me my good grades.

During my freshman year of college, I earned my first F ever in my entire academic career. To be exact, that year I earned a total of three Fs. I still remember checking my first semester grades and thinking, *What am I doing?* How was it possible I had let an entire semester slip by without completing any real work? Those Fs ultimately landed me on academic probation, which included an academic hearing. I was starting to wonder whether I was going to become a lawyer or a criminal because I kept appearing on the offender side of any hearings I attended. It was like déjà vu from high school.

Here I was again allowing my fate to be decided by someone else due to my behavior. I remember sitting on the ground in line in the hallway of the career and planning building, where they were holding the probation hearings, waiting for them to call my name. The line was long. The hallway was lined up with so many young college students discussing why they were there. Some looked concerned and worried, while others laughed as if they were familiar with the process. Either way, we were all in line about to face our fate.

I finally sat face-to-face with a woman who collected the plan and/or promise I had written. Writing a paper on how I planned to improve my grades and maintain them was one of the requirements. The lady quickly explained the conditions of being on academic probation as well as the stipulations to get off of it. She concluded the session by handing me an envelope with a copy of everything she discussed. As if the Fs and academic probation weren't a big enough blow to the gut, I also lost my academic scholarship. I was now financially responsible for paying for college.

My parents had warned me before I had stepped foot on

campus, "We don't have money for college, so thank God you got a scholarship. Make sure you keep your grades up." As I sat in my car, looking at the packet of paperwork, I started realizing I had to stop taking so many bad risks in my life. It was the first time I thought about how my bold, irrational, and sometimes careless behavior was having a negative impact on my life. I had been talking to God all along. However, I hadn't yet mastered hearing or listening to Him. My freshman year at DSU was a reality check for me. I identified some things in me that needed to change.

After sophomore year at DSU, I began to mature; I was officially over the party scene. I was not just focused on improving my grades, but I started to zone in on the next steps of maturity in my life. I started to dig into the college experience and all it had to offer. I took advantage of career planning and signed up for things to help me become a well-rounded young adult. I registered a minor in Spanish, as I thought it would be an asset to be bilingual since I was going to be a lawyer. I began studying for the Law School Admission Test (LSAT). I concentrated more on my criminal justice classes. By junior year, I got into a rhythm that was taking me in the right direction. I still had that bold and outspoken personality, but I was using it for good.

It was during my senior year of college, when I was feeling like I was finally home free, that I found out I was pregnant. *Am I crazy?* I thought. *What am I doing being pregnant my senior year?* I was disappointed in myself. I had already applied to a few law schools. I'd also already taken the LSAT and was awaiting my scores. I remember thinking, *Am I really about to ruin an opportunity I have waited for my entire life?* I'd worked so hard to get to this point. Regardless of how many questions I asked myself, the reality of the situation was that I was about to become a mom.

The summer before my sophomore year at DSU, I had met Kraig. I spent most of my college life dating Kraig, who ended up being the father of my child. I can remember people asking, "Oh, you guys met in college?" We met on the college campus, but he didn't technically go to the school. A lot of guys came on campus to play pickup games of basketball. We began dating and became serious quickly. It didn't take long for us to become an item. I met his mother. He met my parents. I can still remember how he pulled up and brought my mom flowers, which won her over easily. My dad, not so much. He didn't dislike anyone; however, he was a person who only acknowledged actions. He didn't care what good things I said about Kraig, he wanted to see how he lived.

I learned so much about myself in those years with Kraig. What was most obvious was that actions definitely speak louder than words. Our honeymoon period ended quickly, and lies, deceit, and infidelity infiltrated our relationship. We experienced both highs and lows. Unfortunately, so many more lows than highs, but something great came out of our relationship: my daughter, Superia. By the grace of God, I graduated from Delaware State University on May 16, and Superia was born four months later on September 16. I'd planned to attain many titles in my life, but "mother" was never one of them. I was lying in the hospital bed the day I delivered Superia, and my hospital phone rang.

"Hello?" I answered.

"Congratulations, Tiffany, I heard you had a girl." It was my great-aunt Claire. She was my grandmother's sister, a gentle spirit but on fire for God.

"Yes, Aunt Claire, I had a girl," I answered.

"What did you name her?" she asked.

"Superia."

She immediately chuckled. "Niecey, you better be careful what you name her: she might just live up to her name."

Little did I know, Superia would definitely live up to her name.

I started attending church regularly right around the time Superia turned two years old. This was also the time the turmoil between Kraig and I was at its height. My frequent talks with God, which I had started during my college years, increased to talking to God at least three times a day. The job I started after having Superia made it difficult to go to church because I was scheduled to work on Sundays. But anytime I had off on a Sunday, I did not hesitate to get to the house of God.

This was also the same time I bought a home. Kraig and I had decided we would move in together and try the family thing. Living together didn't work at all. I had been warned during the entire home buying process by my dad about living in sin. Though my dad was a man of few words, when he spoke, you listened.

"You can't decide to give your life to God and then move into a house with someone you aren't married to."

We were having the conversation as I moved my things into the townhouse. I had just left the lawyer's office after signing my closing papers. I was too excited about living on my own and was not about to let my dad rain on my parade. I had graduated from college, had bought a new car, was attending church, and I had just bought my first home all within two years. I felt pretty accomplished, and pride wasn't going to let me hear anything that was counter to my decisions.

Here we go, I remember thinking to myself.

I knew how my dad operated. He didn't care about your feelings or if it was the right time. My dad felt like his job as a father was to maintain God's standard in all seasons, which included telling me when I was missing the mark with regard to God. As I continued to move things into the house, he continued talking.

"Tiffany, you just started going to church and strengthening your relationship with God. This isn't going to work."

It didn't take long for reality to set in. It wasn't a full two years after I moved into the house before my finances went down the drain, I lost my car, and I began to lose myself; I finally realized that my dad was absolutely right. Kraig eventually moved out, but we continued our unstable relationship.

The only difference this time from the many other "breakups to make ups" was that Superia was now in the mix, which made things even more complicated. This vicious cycle continued: we got along, we got into a fight, we broke up, and then we got back together. After eight years of playing this game, we finally ended our relationship for good right before Superia turned five years old. We had tried our best to make our family work but accepted that ending our relationship was in the best interest of all parties involved.

Shortly after Kraig moved out, I sold my house, and Superia and I went back to my parents' home to live. This gave me an opportunity to regroup and get myself together. After about a year of paying off debt, reestablishing my credit, and pulling my savings account off of life support, I moved into an apartment with just me and Superia. I began to really embrace my single-parent journey. My mother often told me she couldn't relate to a lot of what I went through, as she had been married before she'd had any of us.

"I couldn't have picked a better man to be your father," I would often hear as we discussed parenthood. However, that didn't stop her from helping me in every way possible. After getting settled in my apartment, I started working a part-time job to supplement my full-time job. I refused to ever let myself get back into a financial bind as I had done after I'd bought my house. Working two jobs resulted in long days. I worked from 8:30 am to 5:00 pm, changed into my part-time job clothes, and worked from 5:30 pm until about midnight most nights. My mom would stay at the apartment with Superia so she could be home in her own bed to sleep. My mom didn't want me picking Superia up so late, breaking up her sleep, and having to get up early the next morning to go to day care. My second job allowed me to stack money, as I was trying to put myself in the best possible financial position to buy another house. I also wanted to start saving money, as Superia was going to be starting school soon. Since Superia's birthday was in September, she missed the cutoff for kindergarten (August 31) and wouldn't start school until the age of six. I took full advantage of my part-time job, as it was good pay with shift differential. I even worked some overnight shifts when available. The times I worked overnight, Superia stayed with my parents, and I would pick her up in the morning.

I recall one morning, after working overnight, I decided to still go to church. I was in the stage of my life where I was rebuilding Tiffany, and the only way I could even begin to do that was through spending time with God. Therefore, the last thing I wanted to do during this stage was miss church. After working overnight, I came up with what I thought was a great plan. Since I got off early in the morning, I would cook dinner early. Then, by the time I cooked dinner and got dressed, it would be time to go to church. My body was still not used to overnights because I didn't work them consistently. I only worked them when my supervisors were in dire need.

I got home from picking Superia up from my parents'

house and began preparing food. I turned the stove on, trying to get dinner done early. I showered and threw on some comfy clothes until I needed to get dressed for church. I checked on the food that was cooking, and everything was going as planned. I decided I would relax for just a few minutes because I still had plenty of time before church started. *Let me lie across this bed, watch a little TV, and relax,* was the last thing I remember thinking before I woke up to a frantic five-year-old screaming, "Mommy! Wake up! The food is burning!" I quickly jumped up and ran into the kitchen and began turning off my pots and pans that were spilling over. Thank God nothing caught fire. I had lain down to rest my eyes and had fallen asleep for over an hour. Needless to say, we ate out that night and missed church.

During this stage in my life, I remember one distinct thing—I was exhausted. I wasn't just physically exhausted from working both jobs, I was also emotionally and mentally exhausted from being a single mother and trying to always figure it out. The mother title comes with so many demands, but being a single mother takes it to another level. As a single mother, you are responsible for everything. And I mean absolutely everything. You are missing the other half being there to share the many burdens. I was always taught that if you have to choose which bills to pay on time, pay your rent or mortgage on time. You always need a roof over your head. Therefore, most times the first bill I would take from would be the cable bill or I'd cut down on the grocery bill.

I was constantly creatively moving money around to make ends meet. If you aren't creatively moving money around, you are trying to arrange transportation and figure out how your child will be dropped off and picked up to and from day care. If you aren't doing that, you are getting your child dressed only to realize nothing fits and they have grown out of everything from clothes to shoes. If that's not the case, you are obsessing that you are being the best parent you can be, given the circumstances.

Once Superia started school, my to-do list grew even more. Now I was checking book bags to sign folders, looking over schoolwork to make sure assignments were getting done, or investigating birthday party invitations to figure out who my child was considering a friend. *Does Superia know her bus number? Is she doing well socially at school? Am I being too hard on her? Am I not being hard enough on her?* As a single parent, you often struggle with trying to find the perfect balance between being a nurturer and a disciplinarian. You do not just care about getting everything done, but you are also focused on getting everything done right. I know one of the things I promised myself was that Superia would not miss out on anything in life simply because she came from a single-parent household. I didn't care how much I had to work, how many jobs I had to take, or how late I had to stay up, my child was not going to be slighted or miss out because she only had her mom in the household. It only takes one time of telling your child "No, I can't afford to this time" or "No, I am not able to do it this time." When you see the disappointment in their face, you decide you don't ever want to experience that type of guilt again. So I overworked myself to make sure that response didn't happen again.

This single-mother journey was weighing on me; I was starting to feel the burden. It also increased my desire to hear from God and to be in God's presence, which caused me to seek God even more. I acknowledged at this point that sporadically visiting churches was not going to suffice. I had frequently attended a church back when Kraig and I were nearing the end of our relationship together. The church had been everything I'd needed at the time.

During that period, Kraig, Superia, and I were living as a family unit. I realized that was around the time I started really losing myself because of all the changes and transitions that had taken place all at once: graduating from college, becoming a mom, moving out of my parents' house, and living with my boyfriend. As my dad said, God had sparked a fire in me right after I'd had Superia, which had gained momentum until I moved in with Kraig and started living in sin. I stopped consistently going to church, and I started thinking everything I was doing was because of my own strength. I had become lost because I had become weak spiritually. If you don't know who you are or where you belong, ask God, because who knows the creation better than the Creator? I needed to strengthen my relationship with God. I started to get back on track with the church search as soon as I moved back home with my parents. I was determined to find a church home; I needed to build a solid foundation in Christ. I needed a church to call home. The church I had been most frequently and consistently attending, Greater Life Christian Church (GLCC), appeared to be the one.

• chapter 2 •

Finding My Faith

*A*t GLCC, God placed leaders over my life who truly began to mold me. I began to mature in all areas of my life, but I grew exponentially in God. I had witnessed a strong foundation in God growing up with two Christian parents. Knowing the truth was one thing, but it was another thing to live it. I began to line up all areas of my life with God's standard to the best of my ability. I began to consistently pray. I began to do more than read the Word; I began to study God's Word. I was careful about what I did day-to-day as well as who I surrounded myself with. I was more cautious about what I participated in. My frequent visits to the bars with friends ceased. I listened to more gospel music than secular music. And I read my Bible almost every night before I went to bed.

This change didn't happen overnight. Around 2008,

when Superia was about five, God began a work in me that everyone around me started to notice. My family, friends, and coworkers began to witness the change. I was far from perfect, but anyone who knew me knew I was working on something. My relationship with God became my priority, and it was evident. I was building and developing a genuine and intimate personal relationship with God.

GLCC members were like a second family to me. I was drawing closer to God, and because of that change, I learned to recognize His voice. It wasn't some ominous voice that sounded like thunder. It was more like quiet, subtle urgings. "Tiffany, you want to go out, have a drink, and chill?" was a constant invitation from friends. And I could quietly hear God say no. It's almost like the moment you surrender to God, your conscious wakes up, and before every little thing you do, you first assess it to determine if it is the right or the wrong thing to do. I knew exactly when it was God speaking. Recognizing God's voice taught me how to be accountable to Him. It caused me to become obedient to God. For some reason, when things are going fine in the life of a Believer, we tend to get lackadaisical with God. "I can miss Bible study tonight because I'm tired," or "I can miss this Sunday because God knows my heart." All of that is true to an extent, but we have to know the times when we are not spiritually strong enough to miss anything regarding God.

As I began to rebuild my relationship with God, I was able to clearly see God's path for my life. So many things in my life began to change because I changed. The first thing that changed was my mindset about being single. I complained so much about being a single mother, I began to get on my own nerves. There was no way in the world I could connect with another man for a relationship when I had so many of my own issues I needed to resolve first. I started embracing my singleness.

Another area I needed to work on was how I responded to life. I realized I needed to work on how I handled things; I had a bad attitude. I began to work on being less impulsive and less emotional. I tried not to say or do anything while I was mad, sad, frustrated, or tired. Yet the greatest change that God opened my eyes to was my career. My career change confirmed that God was definitely working in my life.

As long as I could remember, I had wanted to be a lawyer. However, the longer I remained in the criminal justice system, the more obvious it became that what I wanted wasn't what God had purposed for my life. Everyone who knows me knows I have always desired to be a lawyer. I had expressed the desire to represent or advocate for vulnerable populations around age ten. After some research, I decided I didn't want to be a defense attorney at all. How would I be able to represent someone who may have done something horrific to a child? I decided I wanted to work for the state, so I changed my direction from wanting to be a defense lawyer to wanting to become a prosecutor. I remember anytime anyone brought up anything referencing the criminal justice system or anything regarding the law, I would weigh in on the conversation.

Initially, my intentions were to go to law school immediately after college and get started on my legal career. However, with Superia due the September following my senior year of college, it was impossible. This slight delay did not dim the passion and fire I had for law school, but it made me think there could be an alternate route I needed to take. I believed God had set up this alternative route for me to gain more knowledge and insight about the criminal justice system and how it worked from beginning to end before entering into it. This would give me the opportunity to understand how the system worked and to be able to see the whole picture before I stepped into my law career.

From 2003 to 2007, I worked in many capacities with regard to the criminal justice system. I worked with inmates in a behavior modification program at the James T. Vaugh Correctional Center (JTVCC) in Smyrna, Delaware. I worked for a company called Civigenics, which held a contract with what the JTVCC called the Crest Program. The Crest Program was a short-term, in-prison program focused on behavior modification for inmates who were about to transition out of prison to a work-release program. I was a counselor in the program and managed a caseload of inmates. Even though this was the lowest paying job I ever held after attaining my degree, it was the most rewarding. I learned how to deal with all types of people from all types of backgrounds who had all types of beliefs. Not only was I teaching these guys, but I was also learning from them.

One of my job duties as a counselor was to teach prosocial behavior, or life skills, in the program; there was a twelve-week cycle to cover twelve different life skills. There was one particular class I remember like it was yesterday. I'm not sure which skill I was teaching, but the conversation that took place during this particular class will always resonate with me. As a counselor in the program, I was basically in the same quarters as the inmates. When I taught classes, I went on the "pod," which housed about twenty-five to thirty inmates; I taught in their living quarters. I can remember sitting among the group and one of the inmates saying, "Pain has a short memory." I was a twenty-two-year-old fresh college graduate and new single mother: I didn't have a lot of life experience yet.

He said, "Think of something that you did that may have hurt physically, but you continued to do it anyway. Maybe you rode down a hill really fast and fell off and scraped your skin on the cement. It hurt for that moment, maybe a couple of minutes, but as soon as the pain went away, so did the painful memory. How long did it take before you got back on the bike and rode it again? Not long, huh? How quickly we forget how painful something is when the pain is gone, and yet we are so quick to do it again."

At the end of this particular class, we concluded as a group that life will never be without pain. You just have to make sure your pain is not wasted; you must make sure your pain is connected to your purpose. Pain should motivate you, push you, and change you for the better. If pain doesn't birth change or produce fruit, it is pointless pain, and that kind of pain tends to have a short memory. Since pointless pain is short-lived, most of the time it will cause you to repeat the same detrimental behavior, putting you right into a vicious cycle.

I never forgot that conversation we had in that class. It has stuck with me for eighteen years, as I am now forty years old. It resonated with me for a few reasons. The ultimate reason was that it taught me how to categorize pain. I learned to tell the difference between purposeful pain and pointless pain. After the class, I remember thinking to myself, *What pain have I caused myself for no reason or for being disobedient to God in my life that didn't amount to anything good, and what pain has God allowed in my life for His purpose?* Having the invaluable opportunity to deal with various types of people from diverse racial and cultural backgrounds in this position quickly grew me as a counselor and even more so as an adult in my natural life. The greatest benefit was that I opened up my spiritual ears. Talking to God is great, but being able to hear God talk to you brings about a different perspective. In less than two years, I was promoted from counselor to senior counselor. I finally found my rhythm in that position, and at the same time, I began to desire more of God.

I wanted to start going to church on a regular basis. This position made the task difficult, as my schedule ran from

Sunday to Thursday. I began to try and barter with God. I made a deal with Him. If He made a way for me to leave the prison job and find a job where I only worked weekdays, I would give my Sundays to him. That was my promise to God, and I meant it wholeheartedly. It was that very moment that I recognized I needed my plan to actually line up with God's will for my life. God knew just what He was doing, and He wanted me spending time with Him.

Soon after my prayer request, I got a new job as the first drug court case manager for Court of Common Pleas in Kent County, Delaware, for misdemeanor drug charges. In this new position, I learned how to deal with recovering addicts who were court ordered to complete the program. The program included random urine screen analysis for drug tests, weekly life skill classes, and reporting to court for updates on their status in the program. Through my work at drug court, I had constant interaction with the state or prosecutor's office. Being in court every week allowed for me to get to know court personnel as well as the prosecutors. They often complimented me on a job well done.

One day in court, one of the prosecutors who knew my future plans came to me and said, "You are always prepared in court, you send over everything to our office in a timely manner, and you know how to call the calendar in court on your own. Since I know you desire to go to law school, why don't you come work with us? We have an admin support position available in the criminal unit you should apply for. I will have no problem giving you a reference." After a positive interview process, I got the job as an administrative assistant at the prosecutor's office, Delaware Department of Justice, Kent County. I remember thinking that God had planted me in the right spot at the right time, and now was the time to get back on track for law school.

The first day I stepped into the Department of Justice (DOJ), I was confident that the next stop for me was going to be law school. I definitely brought some flavor to the DOJ. I noticed I was the only Black employee in the Superior Court Unit of Criminal Division at the Department of Justice. However, that didn't stop them from becoming family to me. I started as secretarial support in the Rape Unit and then became secretarial support in the Drug Unit where I managed what we called the ME, or Medical Examiner, list for drug evidence.

While at the prosecutor's office, I completed a certification in legal studies, which allowed me to be promoted to paralegal. In 2009, I was the first African American paralegal in Felony Screening Unit: Criminal Division. I learned how to prepare a case for a murder trial; how to manage and document items on an asset forfeiture list; and how to redact victim, witness, and defendant statements. I also went to court to assist the prosecutors during preliminary hearings. I was learning so much about the criminal justice system while at the prosecutor's office. There was no better time to apply for law school, having extensive work experience under my belt and opportunities to get exceptional recommendations from various criminal justice personnel.

I prepared all of my documents such as transcripts, LSAT scores, and recommendation letters and uploaded everything on the Credential Assembly Service, formerly known as Law School Data Assembly Service. I remember feeling so accomplished and ready to get back on track. I had even started inquiring about summer classes at the law school I applied to so I could get a head start once I received a confirmation that I was accepted. That very same week, as I was sifting through a police report, I heard God clearly say, "You are going to teach." This thought was so far-fetched and off base from anything I had ever desired to do that I immediately realized it could only have been from God. My dad was a former teacher, and he had suggested becoming one while I was in college. I had quickly told him no because "I don't even like kids."

I decided I wasn't going to fight this voice because I knew it was God. I immediately answered the call by getting online and searching for local graduate-level education programs since I already had an undergraduate degree. I looked for education programs that I could start immediately. Everything fell into place, from my master's degree application fee being waived to my classes fitting perfectly around my work schedule. My advisor in education explained that because I had no education background at all, I was responsible for taking a few undergraduate courses as prerequisites before taking some of the master's level courses. He advised me that it would take approximately two years to complete the coursework and I needed to build an extra three months in for student teaching. I finished all the required coursework for my graduate degree in education in seventeen months. Therefore, next on my list to complete was student teaching.

· chapter 3 ·

All Roads Lead to Education

I began teaching in 2012 at Central Middle School (CMS) as a student teacher. I can still remember when I walked in to meet my "cooperating teacher," the person who would be supervising me and mentoring me throughout the student teaching. I made sure I was dressed professionally, as that was my dress attire for the prosecutor's office anyway. The lady in the main office seemed irritated that I was there so early during what I learned was one of the busiest times in a school, a few weeks before school was scheduled to start. There were boxes everywhere, and everyone was dashing in and out of the office, asking questions, checking the status of orders, and making small talk with this lady. She didn't give too much attention to anyone. She answered questions without even looking up; you could tell she was more focused on getting her work done without interruptions.

When I arrived, she looked surprised. I was scheduled to be at the school at 7:30 am. I was there around 7:15 am.

"Does your teacher know you are coming?" she asked in an irritated manner.

"Yes, ma'am," I answered.

"Well, you are going to have to sit over there and wait until she gets here. You are here early," she barked and went back to her work. I sat there for maybe another ten minutes until a middle-aged white woman came through the office and said, "Are you Tiffany Smith?"

I excitedly jumped up.

"Yes!" I said and started walking toward her with my briefcase in hand as if I had won a spot as a contestant on a game show.

She said, "Come with me." She had a very outgoing and friendly personality. As we walked to her classroom, which was right across from the office, she kept looking at me as if she was trying to figure something out. When we got to her classroom door, she put the key in the door to unlock it but first turned around and faced me.

"Did you go to Dover High School?" she asked.

Dover High School, I said to myself. *Oh no!* Anytime someone referred to my high school years, I got nervous, as those years were filled with memories of rebellion. I cautiously answered, "Yes."

She said, "Did you have Mrs. Vaughan for math?"

Oh no, I thought again. I did have Mrs. Vaughan for Algebra 1 and Algebra 2, but did I want to admit this to her?

"Yes," I cautiously answered again.

"I knew I remembered you! I went by my maiden name then. I was her long-term substitute when she went out on maternity leave. I remember you walking out of the class after being slightly disruptive. I remember you were good at math but did not want to be bothered with me as the long-term substitute. You made it clear you were only interested in being taught by Mrs. Vaughan. It was my first year teaching."

I stood there really at a loss for words.

"Yes, I was a handful in high school," I muttered. Just that easily, something that had happened years ago had resurfaced in my life. And if that wasn't enough, right then her co-teacher called to touch base with her for the day. My cooperating teacher kindly explained to her over the phone that they would be hosting a student teacher.

"A student teacher? You have to be kidding me!?" was all I could hear, with a few obscenities added. I sat at the student desk and for a second began questioning if this move was actually the right move.

After a rocky start to my first day of student teaching, my cooperating teacher began to review the basics of middle school with me. I was very familiar with middle school, especially CMS because I had attended CMS for seventh and eighth grade. Middle schools are often set up in a team model with one expert teacher to instruct in each content area. A math teacher, a science teacher, and an English language arts teacher make up a middle school team. I was placed on an eighth-grade team where I assisted my cooperating teacher who was a special education teacher.

A special education teacher's primary responsibility is to support the students with disabilities or who have an Individualized Education Plan (IEP). This made the most sense since my master's degree was in the area of special education. I was specifically given a handful of students who had IEPs to focus on and who also had plenty of personality. I quickly became one of the go-to people on the team for behaviors and dealing with classroom disruptions and "girl drama." One reason was because I didn't have a class of my own: I wasn't the content teacher or officially a special education teacher. Since I was only a student teacher, I had more available time than any of the other teachers on the team. My previous work experience and background in behavior modification gave me the upper hand when dealing with behaviors. I had a positive and strong influence on the students, especially my strong-minded girls. Most of the time, I felt like a counselor more than a teacher, but being in that position, I learned so many valuable things that no book or class could have taught me. Not only did I learn how to write IEPs, how to support students with disabilities, and the importance of classroom management, I also learned how powerful relationships are in regard to middle school students. As the last week of student teaching began to draw near, I received almost thirty letters from the eighth graders about how much they appreciated me, loved me, and how I had made such an impact on their lives.

"Ms. Smith, can't you just stay for the rest of the school year?" one of my eighth-grade girls asked on my last day. By the end of my student teaching stint, I recognized that I was finally walking in my purpose. All these years I'd had this detailed plan for my life, I'd had my own will for my life, and not once did I ever consult God to see if it was what He wanted or had purposed for my life.

The next decision had to be one of the biggest and most difficult decisions I've ever made. I started to ponder the thought of not returning to the prosecutor's office at all. I had technically been on a leave of absence since September 1, 2012, which allowed me to secure my job, use my vacation time to get paid, and maintain health insurance for me and Superia. It became so evident that God was in this career change, especially when I had gone to my immediate supervisor at the Department of Justice to initially request the leave of absence for student teaching. He'd answered, "I have no problem approving it, but I'm not sure if the attorney general (who happened to be Beau Biden at the time) is going to approve it." Usually, the only time you were allowed to request a leave of absence was for medical reasons, mental health reasons, and/or to advance your career in the legal field, such as going to law school or doing a law clerkship. I wasn't so sure the attorney general was going to approve me going to student teach, which indicated that I would soon be leaving the legal field and obviously the department to become an educator. Beau Biden approved my leave of absence. This only solidified what I already knew was true: God is sovereign, and He can use anyone and anything to fulfill His plan, purpose, and will for my life as long as I yield to Him.

The DOJ had approved my leave of absence through October 31, 2012. At that time, I was supposed to return to the prosecutor's office as a paralegal, graduate, and then try to get a job. The amount of time approved for my leave of absence posed a problem. Even though my leave of absence was to end October 31, I wasn't set to complete student teaching until November 30, 2012.

I had a decision to make. I could either resign at the prosecutor's office to complete the final month of student teaching so I could complete my master's degree in special education or go back November 1 and put off finishing student teaching, which meant putting off getting my master's degree. I had been praying and speaking to God for weeks, asking Him for guidance. I needed God to speak to me about my next move so it wouldn't be the wrong one. I needed to make the right decision according to God's will for my life. One thing about God is that He gives us free will. In life, you always have two options: do what you want to do (free will), or surrender your free will and do what God wants you to do (God's will).

As the last day of my leave of absence drew closer, I sought

God even more. On Sunday, October 28, I went to church as I did every Sunday. When it was time for the sermon, my pastor said, "If I had to choose a title for today's message, it would be Don't Miss the Moment!" As I sat there in my pew, looking around as if God was sitting somewhere in the congregation, I almost couldn't believe what I was hearing. I don't know if God could have given me a clearer sign than the one that came across the pulpit that Sunday. I wrote my letter of resignation that week, thanking the Department of Justice for the opportunity and for the almost six years of love, learning, and support.

November 1, 2012, I resigned from the prosecutor's office and was officially unemployed. I remember thinking, *How could I possibly return to being support staff at the Department of Justice after such a rewarding experience in the school?* After you get a glimpse of God's will for your life, it is a true struggle to return to the plan you had for yourself.

Leaving the prosecutor's office was bittersweet. Despite the excitement that was brewing in me regarding the new opportunity I was being afforded to change lives through education, I was still hesitant. Unfortunately, one of my best characteristics is that I am a loyal person. Sometimes I become loyal to the extent that it's not beneficial for me; I feel obligated to stay, whether in a friendship, in a relationship, or at a job.

My loyalty can be a gift and a curse. As I began to grow

in God, I realized the only person that I needed to be loyal to was God. Being loyal to God is the only way we can keep from being disappointed. Not that God grants every petition or prayer request. Thank God He doesn't, as we sometimes don't know what's best for ourselves. God is faithful to His word and, therefore, keeps His promises. Who else or what else can guarantee that?

Regardless of God's faithfulness, I was hesitant. I was going to miss the amazing group of people I had grown to love, and I also felt a sense of guilt for leaving after everything they had done for me. They had done everything imaginable to support me in my law school endeavors as well as in my personal life being a single mother. The memory of them assembling my daughter's motorized scooter I bought for her one Christmas and test driving it around the office is only one of many memories showing their continued love and support for me.

Though everything appeared to be falling into place, there was one minor detail that still needed to be worked out. Maybe it wasn't actually a minor detail but a pretty significant one. I didn't actually have a job to go to if I resigned from the prosecutor's office. I was about to give up a tenured state position, where I had great work relationships and work history, to wait for a job to become available in education.

I second-guessed myself almost immediately, wondering if I had made the right decision. The Bible teaches us that when we do things under instruction from God solely because we trust Him, it helps us build our faith. The more we build our inner man, the more we will walk in the Spirit or under the instruction of God. You can always tell when you are allowing God to lead you because it does not feel good; it fights with your emotions and your flesh. The flesh is always contrary to God's Spirit. In the Bible, Galatians 5:17 reads, "For the flesh lusteth against the Spirit, and the Spirit against the flesh: and these are contrary the one to the other: so that ye cannot do the things that ye would." God's Word gave me assurance that I had made the right decision because my flesh was speaking to me loud and clear: *Are you crazy?*

I am going to be honest: doing what God says to do doesn't usually come easy. I questioned over and over if I had made the right decision. I naturally began to look at my situation. I had no job, no money, and no real plan except that I knew I needed to land a teaching job. It was November, which was not an ideal time to find a teaching job. There were currently no teaching jobs available in Capital School District, the district where I had done my student teaching. That was a problem because that is where I desired to be. I began preparing all my paperwork for my teaching license to complete my master's degree as well as preparing for graduation. I can remember all of my family and friends being extremely supportive. On a daily basis, my family and friends assured me that a job would soon become available. Then there was everyone else. People who were aware of my situation began asking me questions like "So what are you going to do if you can't get a job soon?" They never asked me if I was out of my mind for quitting a permanent position without another one lined up, but I could discern it in their tone.

In the eyes of this world, I could understand their concern. To them, it didn't make sense; it wasn't logical. It is common knowledge that you never quit a job without having another job lined up. That is a good standard to live by in the world. But what nonbelievers don't realize is, as a Believer, I wasn't necessarily bound by the constraints of the world. As the Scriptures in John chapter 17 verse 16 states, "They are not of the world, even as I am not of the world." Activating my faith as a Believer tells me that, despite what it may look like, God has the power and ability to change the course. And even in times when His will is for you to endure, He gives you grace to do just that.

I was already praying, but I realized I needed to change what I was praying about. I stopped repeatedly asking God for a job. God is all knowing, or what we call omniscient. Obviously, God already knew I needed a job. Instead, I asked God for grace, strength, and power to endure this particular season. I prayed for peace and patience as I waited for God to move. As each day passed and I got closer and closer to graduation, God began to speak to me more frequently. I could hear God asking me over and over again, "Do you trust me? Why go to church, tell people I am the Great I Am, tell them I can do anything but fail, go to Bible study, fast, and pray if you don't truly believe it yourself?" God kept taking me to this Scripture: "Faith without works is **dead**" (James 2:20, emphasis added). Faith is doing and believing despite what it may look like to the natural eye. In order to exercise your faith, you have to operate *from* a place in victory instead of working to get *to* a place of victory. This doesn't mean that we as Believers always win in our eyes. It means that no matter what God allows to take place in our life, even if He doesn't do what we ask, we praise and worship Him because we know He can. If He doesn't, we accept His response for the time being and learn to withstand whatever He allows to happen in our life.

True faith is believing and trusting God despite what you see with your natural eye. True faith is trusting and believing God in spite of what the outcome may be. I quit a position without another one lined up but not before consulting God. I had to step out in faith and believe and trust His word, and that's exactly what I did. I needed to show God that I trusted Him. So I put myself in a position where He could be the only solution. God informed me that He had to do it His way. He assured me that I was going to get a job at the appointed time, and when I did, man would not be able to take credit for it. When it did happen, there would be no doubt that it was all God. Too often, we want the glory for making things happen when all the glory belongs to God.

On January 13, 2013, I graduated with a master's degree in special education. On January 27, 2013, I started my new position as a seventh-grade special education teacher at Central

Middle School, the same school where I had completed my student teaching, the school I had attended, and the district I desired to be in. Once again, God showed that He was faithful to His word. If God said it, then it will come to pass. This entire situation increased my level of faith.

chapter 4

Recognizing My Purpose
in Education

I spent the rest of the 2012–2013 school year and the following 2013–2014 school year as a seventh-grade special
education teacher at CMS. The next year, my principal placed
me in eighth grade as a special education teacher. I was back
on team with the same teachers I had originally done my
student teaching with. Then, not even three weeks into the
school year, my principal called me on a Friday shortly after
school was over. She informed me that she had just checked
my account in the Delaware Educator Data System, which
is a database that stores all your certifications and teaching
licenses as an educator. She had noticed that I was certified
in middle school math. I had obtained that certification
because it was one of the requirements for the completion of
my master's degree. If you majored in special education, you

also had to be certified in a content area such as ELA, math, science, or social studies. Since the university I had attended had this requirement, I had chosen math. I had always loved math and had been pretty good at it in high school. Before I completed my master's degree, I took the Praxis test in middle school math and passed it.

Anyway, my boss called me to inform me that one of the math teachers on another team had accepted a different position in the building, and she wanted me to think about taking over his position. I sat on the other end in silence because I was stunned. "Pray on it and talk to me on Monday" were her exact words, as she knew I was a Believer, and she was one too. She implied that she would be looking for an answer on Monday as if she was actually asking. I soon realized this was more of a "voluntold" situation, or in other words, she was going to place me where she wanted.

Monday, I started moving my stuff across the building to get set up for my new position on my new team. Everything happened so quickly. The questions didn't start flooding my mind until I began moving from my old classroom to the new one. I had only ever been a special education teacher, which meant I was always in the room with another teacher. Having two adults in the classroom made life easier for so many obvious reasons. I was able to consult and get input from another adult when making decisions about students' instruction, behavior, and well-being.

However, in this new position, I was the general education

teacher, or content teacher. As a special education teacher, I had ensured that students' IEPs were being followed. However, in this position, my primary job was to teach math. I finally settled in with my new eighth-grade team, but I initially didn't feel welcomed at all. The math teacher before me had been there for a while. The team was happy he'd gotten the job he desired, but they weren't happy about the fact that he was no longer on team with them. What I learned immediately after becoming a teacher was that we don't like change.

Despite the fact that education is constantly changing, change usually comes with much resistance. Teachers are creatures of habit and routine. They don't like any type of disruption to their norm. I was teaching content I had never taught before, I wasn't sure I even wanted to teach it, I didn't know how great I'd be at it, with a team who wasn't excited about my arrival, and the school was piloting a new math curriculum all at the same time. Since the school was piloting new curriculum, there were no formal lesson plans; I had to build new lesson plans for each unit. I spent hours every night preparing the lesson as well as learning how to present the instruction. It was one thing to know the content—I knew the math. However, it was another to know how to teach the content, which is pedagogy.

Throughout my school career, there were plenty of teachers who were obviously intelligent and knew their content but were horrible teachers. It wasn't until third marking period of that school year in my new position that

I got into a rhythm. I was learning what to do and what not to do in math dealing with middle school students. And I must admit I was proud of myself. Not only did I recall how much I enjoyed math, but I also discovered I was good at teaching it. I knew how to deliver the instruction. I could base this assumption on the quality of work I was getting from my students.

Though all of this was a major win, there was an even bigger takeaway—the glaring and obvious realization that I absolutely loved middle school students, especially eighth-grade students. The students on the team I was teaching on were known for their "personality," for lack of a better word. To give you context of the term "personality," there were seven fights on the team the first four weeks of school, one of them being in the library while I was administering one of my formal baseline tests; the students stood up in the middle of testing and started fighting.

These students molded me, to say the least. They challenged me in areas I couldn't imagine. They made me put my money where my mouth was; they made sure I was the person I claimed to be. Could you love a student the next day after they cursed you out? Could you continue to daily encourage a student who never listened to your directives and did what they wanted despite your constant plea to comply with the rules? Could you love a student who barely loved themselves? I realized why I was going to be amazing at this teaching thing. Not because I was some math genius who knew everything about math, not because I'd worked in behavior modification before and could manage behaviors well, and not because I could write lesson plans better than most. These students pulled out of me one of God's greatest gifts: love.

And not just loving my job and what I did; it was deeper than that. I was able to genuinely love children I didn't birth. I had an unconditional love for these students like I did my own biological daughter. This love allowed me to reach them while others could not. I knew how to hold them accountable. I knew when to hold them accountable. I knew how to hold them to a standard of excellence and push them to higher heights despite each of their personal circumstances. I had three core values I used to govern my classroom as a teacher: I loved them, respected them, and protected them. Each one of those values was equally important. I left the criminal justice system because I realized I wanted to do something preventative, or before the fact, instead of reactive, or after the fact.

I also recognized and understood the power of education. I realized that if I'd had caring teachers who went the extra mile when I was in high school, things could have been different for me as a teenager. If someone would have taken a moment to sit me down and actually have a genuine talk with me, so many of the negative outcomes I experienced in high school could have been eliminated. And who knows, things may have turned out differently. Unfortunately, most young adults and students, including myself while I was in high school, fail to realize that there is power in knowledge. So, until students develop a desire to learn, an educator must be strategic. I focused on empowering all students who were in my classroom until they began to develop or grasp the "knowledge is power" concept.

I used one rule of thumb before I did anything regarding a student. I would ask myself one question when I was unsure how to proceed in a situation: *Would I do this same thing or want this same thing done to my own daughter in these circumstances?* That maxim kept me accountable as an educator. It kept me grounded and reminded me of the constant grace and mercy God continues to extend to me. So often in life, God gives us grace, rewards us with things we don't deserve (time, possessions, jobs, or any desire), and withholds consequences or punishment when it could be justified (this is called mercy) because He loves us unconditionally and in spite of ourselves. This perspective kept me humble and ensured that I loved my students against all odds. I didn't care about their race, gender, socioeconomic status, who their parents were or were not, or if they liked me or couldn't stand me. I loved them all the same.

In 2017, I was awarded Central Middle School Teacher of the Year. I continued to teach math, earning recognition and awards for best growth data for Delaware's state testing, Smarter Balanced Assessment Consortium, three years in a row. I learned how to grow students in a subject they initially told me they hated when they first walked through my classroom door.

As I entered my fourth year of teaching math, my principal came to me again with another challenge. She advised me that she wanted me to take on an Honors Algebra 1 course. Normally, a middle school teacher wasn't allowed to teach a high school course without a high school certification; I only had a middle school math certification. I had a few hesitations with this proposal. In the past, the majority of the students I'd worked with were students who weren't proficient, or on grade level, or weren't the easiest to manage with regard to behavior in the classroom. This posed a different kind of challenge. However, I accepted the second voluntold assignment from my principal for what I didn't know at the time would be my last year in the classroom.

chapter 5

New Assignments in Education

In some ways, I was dreading my first year having an Honors Algebra 1 group. This wasn't because I was worried about dealing with the students at all. Instead, I felt like all eyes were on me. My principal had spoken to the higher-ups at the district about the situation, and they were somewhat hesitant about allowing me to teach the honor students. They were hung up on the fact that I wasn't high school certified. They also brought up the previous trend in data that showed there was a lack of growth for the high achieving students with regard to formal testing, and they weren't sure I was prepared for the challenge. These students were already proficient, or on grade level or higher, and it was usually a true task to get them to grow in the "green," or increase to a higher proficiency level, which usually meant they needed to reach above grade level. I appreciated my principal's faith in me, but to be honest, I wasn't thrilled with or interested in this task.

The problem was that when my principal saw a change that needed to take place that would benefit students, she was going to make sure it happened, despite whether you desired to do it or not. It wasn't that I didn't love teaching math or that I didn't love all students; I knew these students were going to have to be taught in a different way. The only honors kid I had any experience with was my own child, Superia. She had been in Gifted and Talented Education since elementary school and continues to take Advanced Placement courses even now as a high school student. She never asked me for help with anything, so I wasn't even sure what her academic struggles were or if she had any at all. She was intrinsically motivated and always figured out things for herself. So, technically, I had no experience.

I walked in the first day of school for the 2018–2019 school year, and thirty-one students were sitting in their seats quietly and attentively. I remember thinking, *Where did these kids come from?* I know this sounds bad, but I hadn't realized we had such compliant kids in our middle school. I was used to students who were a little less compliant and slightly difficult to manage; I was used to students with a bit more personality or attitude. The first few weeks were a struggle trying to find the best routine and rhythm for my new scholars. They were eighth graders who were identified as advanced and were placed in a ninth-grade algebra course. The first instructional red flag was that they had gone from seventh grade to ninth grade and had not taken eighth-grade math, which is foundational for algebra. Eighth-grade students were usually taught pre-algebra to set the tone for algebra courses. I had to find a way to teach both eighth-grade math (pre-algebra) and algebra together. I had the students for an hour-and-a-half block. I tried to split the class by spending an hour on algebra and thirty minutes on pre-algebra. That didn't work. Then I tried to use half the class time for algebra and the other half for pre-algebra. That didn't work either.

It wasn't until about four weeks in that I realized my way wasn't working. I couldn't just stop in the middle of instruction and shift to another direction, which was exactly what I had been doing. I needed to approach this class in a different way. I prayed about it and asked God to guide me. I needed God to point me in the right direction. The first thing He brought to my attention was that I was controlling everything. I didn't need to control everything with these students because they were intrinsically motivated and wanted to do well for themselves.

Finally, by the middle of the fourth week, I sat on the desk in front of them and said, "Okay, scholars, this is not working. I need input and insight from all of you. What am I doing right? What am I doing wrong? How can we improve our learning environment?" We had dialogue for about fifty minutes. This wasn't any ordinary talk: these students were very perceptive.

Not only did they give insight on what we should do as a class moving forward, but they also reflected on why what we had done for the past four weeks did not work. We decided that day that we would restructure the entire class, and that's exactly what we did. I looked over the eighth-grade and ninth-grade curriculum and combined them.

In education, we can get carried away regarding how much material we cover versus how deep we go into the material. "Breadth vs. depth" is always a topic of discussion in education. The students and I created and constructed a learning environment that impressed me. We combined curriculum and fostered an environment where the students did the leading. They led warm-ups, classroom discussion, and reflection on each lesson. They created an environment where having a wrong answer was an opportunity to help each other. They were so invested in the class because they had created it.

As each day passed in our newly constructed learning environment, I became more of a facilitator than a teacher. We had created such an environment for learning that the class almost seemed to run itself. This allowed me to push these students in ways I hadn't even anticipated. The heights they reached amazed me; these kids were simply amazing. They changed my way of thinking, and in return, I changed their way of thinking. Every day I made a conscious effort to build their confidence. I assisted them with unlearning specific bad habits such as always asking, "Is this right?" I instilled in them that it's not always about getting the right answer or earning an A, but about becoming independent in a classroom, learning to investigate math in different ways, learning how to apply math to the real world, and never giving up despite how difficult it gets. I constantly reminded them that if they wanted more out of anything in life, they had to do more. I reminded them that they deserved to be the best, but it was going to take hard work and working when they didn't feel like it.

Not only did I accomplish the goal to teach a different level of scholars that year, but I learned so much myself. Every year I learn from my students, but this year elicited a different level of growth for me as an educator and even more so as a person. God allowed these students to show me the benefits of humility. God put me in a place where I would be receptive to their feedback. The students showed me that restrictions shouldn't be placed on any student because, in the right environment, they will reach heights you couldn't believe. My honor students reminded me that the classroom truly belongs to the students and that they have just as much say in how things go as I do. They taught me how to be a better listener.

One fundamental thing I learned is that even though the strategies and techniques may have been different at times from my general education students, the algebra students needed the same things as all my other students. They needed someone to love them unconditionally and believe in them. As adults, we sometimes put limitations on our students by assuming they cannot accomplish a task because it's too difficult when that's not the truth. Thank God He doesn't treat His children the way we sometimes treat our students in regard to putting limitations of mediocrity on them. The same logic holds true both in a classroom and in real life. In both our natural life and our spiritual life, limitations are often caused by the environment we create or consequences of what we do. If we raise the bar and provide a more conducive environment for learning as well as resources and support, they will rise to the challenge.

God instructs us to do the same thing. If we petition Him for instruction, read our Bibles, and spend time in His presence, He will provide us with resources and support to rise to any challenge as well. I began to incorporate my newly discovered notions into all my classes, both pre-algebra (general education) and Algebra 1 (honors). It made a world of difference; it changed the math classroom culture for the better.

One of the vivid memories I have with this group of students took place the last week of school that year. Two days before I left my classroom, I glanced back and looked at the classroom door window where almost all 120 students had written messages to me during the last few days students were in the building. Almost every single one of my students had written a message on my window, on my boards in my room, and on the desks (in dry erase pen, of course). All the messages expressed a general theme: how much they learned from me, loved me, and were going to miss me. This had to be one of the most rewarding school years I had at Central Middle School.

At the end of each school year, I solicited feedback from my students on how I could improve as a teacher, but the messages this year meant even more since my position next year was going to be much different, which I was unaware of at the time. I kept worrying about timing, whether this was the time for change since I'd had such a successful school year. I remember calling Foster, my boyfriend at the time, to get his insight on it. He was active military and was stationed at Fort Hood in Texas. I always asked for his insight, as he always put things back into perspective for me spiritually. After speaking to him about everything, I asked myself, *Am I ready to come out of the classroom?* I prayed about it and God didn't send a roadblock, so I determined that He must approve of the move. I was about to be reminded that God's timing is perfect.

For the upcoming 2019–2020 school year, I would be the new Response to Intervention (RTI) coordinator at Central Middle School. This meant I would be coming out of the classroom for the first time after being in a classroom for almost six years. I wasn't sure I was ready, as I loved teaching and being in the classroom with students. I kept in mind the ultimate goal: I would be able to positively influence a larger group of students. In this new RTI position, I would be able to impact a building of 1,000 students instead of just a team of 120 students. At the start of the new school year, I received accolades for my impressive data for four consecutive years at Central Middle School as a math teacher. My last year in the classroom, I exceeded my own data from all the previous years, with 70 percent of my students making their growth goal for state testing. This data included the Honors Algebra 1 students whom the administration had been concerned wouldn't grow since they were already proficient and "in the green." When the data was broken down by section or classes, 86 percent of my honors class cohort met their growth goal. This was the best data in regard to state testing I had ever had while teaching in the building!

I had always been big on looking at my own students' data for math. My new role as RTI coordinator would allow me to look at data through a different lens. Instead of focusing on a classroom perspective, I would instead be looking at data from a building perspective. I would be collecting data from our building via the formal measures of testing we used and then identifying the areas of weakness. I would be grouping the data by grade level so we (instructional staff) could address students' areas of weakness correctly and monitor students to ensure they were improving in those areas. I would be using a Response to Intervention model; I wanted to take a more targeted and intentional approach to remediation for our building because we desired better results.

As soon as the 2018–2019 school year was over, I immediately started working on implementing the master plan that would hopefully improve the middle school. I had my entire summer planned around how I was going to first learn my position and then create and implement a new plan to improve the instructional data for CMS. This also required me to be a learner. I submerged myself into as many professional development opportunities as possible. I was nervous and excited all at the same time about my new endeavor. This new position was going to afford me so many new opportunities in education. I had a lot of learning to do, but first I needed to understand the full picture.

I looked at all the data in both English language arts and math content areas that we had collected from both formal measures of testing: state testing and in-house assessments. I reviewed how many students were proficient, which students were below grade level, and which students were above grade level and grouped them by various subcategories. Based on the data results, I identified the worst areas in each subgroup for both ELA and math. I then grouped them based on their weak areas and created and eventually implemented a system where each weakness was addressed using a targeted intervention. Since I was only an "expert" in math and had minimal knowledge about the other subjects, I needed to read as many articles and books on remediation and the RTI model as possible as well as speak to teachers in that content area, as they were the experts.

Despite still being a ten-month employee, which meant technically I was off during the summer months, I came to the school building almost daily. I was busy putting together spreadsheets on data to review and meeting with the building administration on our school's goals and my plans; everything was coming together. By the time I finally looked up from my work, it was already July. All I could think about was how time was moving too quickly. I still had so many things to figure out and so much work to do. Between working on my master plan and filling my schedule with professional development, my summer was full. My principal, another content teacher, and I ended the week in July doing professional development at a local conference on social-emotional learning. We spent a few days after the conference trying to put together a teacher guide and schedule to implement the new program for the upcoming school year. We finished that Thursday and decided we would pick back up on Monday. Little did I know, God had planned an ultimate detour in my life that I didn't see coming.

chapter 6

The Infamous Day

Sunday, July 21, 2019, is a date I will never forget. The date is fixed in my mind like how the monument is set in DC. It's a point of reference for me. If someone tells me about an event that happened to them in June 2019, I say, "That was a month before it happened." If someone tells me about an event that took place in July 2020, I say, "That was about a year after it happened." That day will forever be memorable for me, and though I may lose small details as time passes, I will never forget how I felt during that stage in my life. I can remember all too well the uneasy, anxious, and unsettling feelings that went through my mind, body, and soul during that period. Though this date comes with a plethora of feelings across a wide spectrum of emotions, both high and low, my emotions were not the biggest takeaway from everything I experienced. Those feelings will never outshine the purpose and what God wanted that day to truly represent in my life. That date marks the day God began renewing my mind, refreshing my soul, and repairing my spirit. Contrary to the natural eye and what many may think, that very day, God was giving me my second wind.

There is one key moment that stands out in my mind from that Sunday morning before everything took place. Before I explain that moment, let me quickly walk you through where I was spiritually at that very moment in time. I had gotten to a point where I had become stagnant in my faith; I was stuck with regard to my walk with God. I had started being rewarded for so many accolades, especially at work, that my mind had shifted. I was starting to believe that all this good stuff that was happening to me was due to my own strength. So, though I was elevating in my natural life, my spiritual life had become stale. The fire I had once had for God was growing dimmer and dimmer. For Superia to ask, "Are we going to church?" on Sundays was huge since that was where we went every Sunday for the past nine years. Her asking me that question was a blatant sign that things had drastically changed in our house spiritually over the past few months.

I was feeling so disconnected from God for a few reasons, but the biggest reason was due to my church leadership. The leadership at my church had changed after my ten years of membership. It wasn't just church for me either, it was deeper than that. It had absolutely nothing to do with the church building; it was what God had molded me into while in this building. It was the powerful experience I continued to have with God while I was there. It wasn't even about the titles I began to collect while a member of the church. I had truly solidified my relationship with God in those ten years. My leaders birthed so much out of me. I was a prayer warrior, getting up early in the morning to intercede, or pray, on the behalf of others. I was a true studier of God's Word, reading my Bible every day and trying to study at least once a week. I had become submissive and had yielded to what God wanted out of my life. I was in a place where I was listening to God; I had become obedient. I had finally started to become spiritually mature in God.

So what I couldn't figure out was that if my anchor was in God and not in people, why was I having such a hard time with this change? Despite how connected we are to God and how much we feed our spirit, there is still a human part of us that almost forces us to incorporate routines and be creatures of habit. This can be both good and bad. There is still that human part of us that embraces familiarity, even when God is telling us it's time for change.

Either way, this new change was difficult for me to process. I was angry. I was frustrated. I was disappointed. What was beginning to become clear that particular Sunday morning was that I was having a hard time processing all my feelings and had become distant from God. I could identify and accept how I was feeling, but I couldn't figure out who

I had these feelings toward. I realized I was mad, frustrated, and disappointed, but with who? Was I angry, frustrated, and disappointed with the leadership that had groomed me because they were leaving or the leadership that was coming in simply because they weren't my old leaders? Were the feelings toward God because He had allowed it, or were these feelings toward myself for not being able to accept the change? On that Sunday morning, the question still remained unanswered. The fact that I was able to identify my feelings but could not truly process them or know where to place them caused such a weight for me. I had been in a stagnant place spiritually since the change had taken place. From the beginning of when the changes began to take place, I had questioned God. The more unanswered questions I generated, the more angry, disappointed, and frustrated I became. And feeling like I had no outlet, as I didn't know who I should blame, made this incident even more difficult to overcome.

Now back to Sunday morning on July 21, 2019. I distinctly remember looking in the mirror to fix my hair. I had already called one of my close friends (whom I considered a sister) and had planned a day at the beach. We shared the same name, but she was considered the "sweet" Tiffany, as I was more assertive. They often called us Sugar and Spice. Of course I was labeled "spice" for my sassy attitude. I hollered into Superia's room to let her know my plans for the beach. She looked up at me and then back down at her phone, saying, "Mom, bring me back something from the boardwalk." I can remember checking the weather online and the weather report saying it was going be the hottest day of the year.

"So, you aren't going to church today?" were Foster's words when we had our daily morning check-in. Almost ashamed to respond, I told him no. Since Superia had already asked me the same question, I knew at this point, God was trying to get my attention. This appeared to be the question of the hour because not going to church was completely out of character for me; you would never catch me anywhere on a Sunday morning except in church. Unfortunately, that hadn't been the case for the past few months.

I had been in a different space since all the changes at church. I was completely out of my element in this space, and I could feel it. I was completely wrong in how I was responding to everything, but I refused to get back in line with God. My thought process at the time was that I was rendering some kind of punishment to God or paying Him back for allowing all these changes. I obviously was completely out of my mind if I thought for a moment that I was contending with a matchless God, but in my small, emotional mind, I felt like it was warranted. My mindset was that God had allowed me to be hurt with the entire change up, so why should I care?

After I hung up with Foster, I continued to do my hair while my R & B music blasted. Despite the music blaring, I could hear God's voice as clear as day: "You need to go to church." For the past ten years, I had grown accustomed to hearing God's voice. I prided myself on having a genuine and personal relationship with my Lord and Savior, and therefore, I knew His voice. When I heard Him give me the directive "You need to go to church," I was in complete shock. I wasn't shocked because God was talking to me, as that was a norm for me, but I was shocked at how piercing the subtle voice was, so much so that I turned around as if I expected Him to be sitting there on my bed. The voice was His normal, gentle voice, but something about that day made it crystal clear as if He was right in the room with me. It was so clear, yet alarming, that I responded out loud in a defiant tone, "I'm not going to church. I hate church."

After Tiffany and I picked up lunch, which was subs and cupcakes for dessert, and gathered the books we were going to read on the beach, we jumped in my car and headed to the beach. We decided to go to the Cape Henlopen beach for a few reasons. Cape Henlopen was closer in proximity to where we lived and had no boardwalk with stores, so we assumed it would be less busy on the hottest day of the year. Boy, were we wrong! We walked across the hot sand, scanning the packed beach to locate a free spot to sit down and start our girls' day. We spent a few hours on the beach, eating, talking, laughing, reading, and taking pictures. We made sure to drink lots of ice water to stay hydrated the entire time. After we had finished our girls' day, we packed up all our stuff and headed back home.

When we arrived back home, sweet Tiffany got her stuff and jumped in her car to head back to her house. I called

Superia on my cell phone from in front of the house to tell her I was going to the grocery store to grab a few things for dinner. I had a roommate staying with me for a short period of time while waiting for the closing date on the house she had purchased. I wanted to ensure there was enough food for Superia and I as well as for her and her girls.

I walked into Redner's grocery store with my list already in my mind. Pork chops were on the top of my list, and as I came to the last item, which was flour to fry the pork chops in, I looked up and noticed a younger white gentleman looking at me. I turned down the baking aisle and grabbed the flour. As I came out of the baking aisle, this same young man was still staring at me, almost as if he knew me, as if he was waiting on something. It was that very moment that I heard a vague popping noise in my head, and I became instantly nauseous. I stopped dead in my tracks, and immediately, that young man walked directly over to me.

He said, "Are you okay?"

At that very moment, I realized I couldn't speak. I couldn't even answer him, so I shook my head. I then began to feel myself losing consciousness as well as my balance. I almost fell right into the young man's arms. He laid me down carefully, and I heard another guy run over and say, "I am an EMT. Get her some water." I began fumbling around in my purse to grab my phone. I needed to call someone; I had to call Superia, who was home waiting for me. I needed to tell her what was happening. At that very moment, my former pastor, whose leadership I had sat under for ten years, said my name. I looked over, and he said, "You are going to be okay, daughter." As I slowly began to lose consciousness, I could hear him telling the guys my name and that I had no health conditions. He then began to pray over me.

At that point, I completely lost consciousness. What's funny is that as Believers we always think we will have time to get it right with God if something unexpected happens. We want to believe that whatever emergency situation we may find ourselves in, God is going to permit us to have some extra moments to make sure we can ask for His forgiveness. We believe we are going to have those few minutes to get it right. Here is some perspective for those of you who believe or live life like you have time: From the moment I felt nauseous to the time I lost complete conscious was maybe four minutes. I didn't use those minutes to ask God for His forgiveness or to make sure I got it right with Him. I used those final minutes trying to figure out what was going on with me, trying to get help, and trying to find my phone to call my daughter. Let me assure you, you don't have time.

· chapter 7 ·

Strokes!?

I only have a few clear memories of the next twenty-four hours. I vaguely remember the ambulance ride and the EMTs calling out my vitals and saying that they hadn't found any drugs in my purse, but that there appeared to be a lot of antidiarrheal medicine. I can remember wanting to say, "I am not on drugs, and I have IBS, thank you very much," but I couldn't talk. I couldn't even focus on exactly what was going on in the ambulance. My mind wouldn't let me. I kept drifting in and out of consciousness.

One of the first clear memories I have is waking up in the hospital looking at my mom. She was sitting right next to my bed saying, "Baby, what happened? What's wrong?" I heard her, but I couldn't respond. One reason was because I was way too drowsy and could barely keep my eyes open, and the other was because I myself had no idea what was happening. My thoughts were foggy, and I couldn't totally grasp what was going on with me or around me. I can remember hearing my mom saying to the hospital staff, "How are we going to figure out what's wrong with her if you keep drugging her with morphine?" I remember everyone helping me get into a wheelchair to go somewhere for testing and having a drunk feeling as my mom and cousin Ursula helped me into the chair. I remember thinking, *Why am I having such a hard time moving around?* I felt like I had minimal control of my body, but I couldn't understand why. All I knew was that something had happened and I was in the hospital.

Superia was sitting next to my mom and dad every time I woke up. She kept saying, "Mom, are you okay?" Out of the sixteen years of her life, I had never seen her look worried. I prided myself on being a parent who never allowed my worries to concern Superia. In the hospital was the first time I had ever seen her look so concerned. I tried to smile and was able to nod yes. She said, "I called Trader Joes to let him know what's going on." Trader Joes was Superia's pet name for Foster. Unfortunately, Foster had just left the States a few weeks before for Korea. He was stationed there for the next nine months to a year.

There were so many doctors and nurses in and out of my room, I could hardly keep tabs. Every hour it seemed like a doctor was introducing himself, what he specialized in, and his team. I would fall asleep, and then another doctor and team would come in. It was a revolving door of doctors. The next memory is one of the first distinct memories I have from the hospital. A woman with a team of doctors walked in.

"We believe we have figured it out," she said. "She had a stroke. Actually, she had a few strokes." I turned toward the doctor and was barely able to get out, "Who, me?!" She confirmed that not only did I have two strokes, but I had a total of eight blood clots in my brain. Six of the blood clots were small enough to move throughout the bloodstream in my brain, but the two larger clots were obstructing blood flow. Those two blood clots were what had caused the strokes. She proceeded to state that a CT scan takes up to eight hours to show a stroke, so that was why we had spent almost five hours in the hospital with no answers, but the MRI had immediately confirmed it.

My mom said, "So she had a few small strokes."

The doctor responded, "They weren't small strokes; they weren't small at all." The doctor continued explaining the severity of the strokes: the entire back of my brain had lost blood flow with all the clots, and the two bigger blood clots had completely blocked blood flow.

My mom asked her, "What caused them?"

The doctor responded, "That's what we are trying to figure out." As I lay in the hospital bed, I just kept replaying her words over and over again in my mind, focusing on the word "strokes." I didn't have one stroke but two strokes, with multiple blood clots present in my brain. The concern in her voice sent a chill down my spine as she advised that the next twenty-four hours were crucial. She warned us that there was a considerable chance of having another stroke within twenty-four hours of the first stroke as well as a chance for seizures.

Superia lay next to me in the bed. I could tell she was so worried.

"Trader Joes keeps calling me and checking up on you. You are always asleep when he calls. He told us not to wake you." She called him on FaceTime so I was able to see him.

"Baby Cakes!" That was his nickname for me. "Don't you worry about anything. God has you. We are going to get through this." I heard him loud and clear. The problem was that I didn't believe everything was going to be okay. The next twenty-four hours were not just a challenge for me physically but even more so mentally. I felt like I was in the world unknown. No one had definitive answers for anything. What I didn't know was that God was about to rebirth something spiritually in me during this period of unknown that I can't even begin to describe in words. See, despite what we don't know, God sees all, hears all, and knows all. God knew exactly what He was doing.

As soon as word got out, visitors from everywhere and anywhere came to see me in the hospital. I felt like I had a non-stop stream of visitation. I even had students calling up to the hospital. At one point, a nurse who walked in with what had to be the fifth bouquet of flowers, said, "Okay, who are you?" It was taking forever for me to process conversations, so this really confused me. I recited my name, thinking she was doing one of the brain checks they did around the clock. Once you have a brain injury, the nursing staff comes in to see how you are progressing by asking you questions like What is your name, When is your birthday, What day is today, and Where are you? The doctors and nurses also do a lot of hand-eye coordination exercises to see how your brain is improving. So, when the nurse who walked in asked, "Who are you?" I thought it was another brain question. She followed up with, "Are you famous? I have never seen such an outpour of love for one person."

Though all the visits, phone calls, and text messages were thoughtful, they were quite draining. I appreciated the immense outpour of love, concern, and support from everyone, but entertaining visitors was a true task. I had a hard time putting my words together to talk. It was even difficult to concentrate on what others were saying to me. Focusing on a simple conversation became daunting. I remember some visits, while other visits I still don't remember. However, my mom, dad, Superia, and Foster (via FaceTime) appeared to be on rotating shifts to monitor me. My brother, who never takes off of work, was there, looking like he was about to fall apart. He didn't do well with things of this nature. My sister, who is a teacher in DC, was calling and getting continual updates throughout the day. My parents didn't want her to come just yet, not until they had a game plan. They told her to stay still.

My cousin Ursula, who is more like a sister, had burned the roads up getting here. She also lived in Maryland and never took off of work, unless it was about family. She didn't play when it came to family. She was present for every emergency situation in our family and remained with the family member until she felt comfortable leaving. The point is that I had a great support system during this time. My family began screening calls and visits, allowing me to get more rest, which the doctors were adamant I needed. Though I needed rest, they also wanted to pinpoint all the parts of my body that had been affected by the stroke. Talking was only one of many things affected.

I had a hard time walking as well. I was a fall risk and could barely balance myself to walk. Therefore, I was not allowed out of the bed without calling the nurse for assistance. But I got tired of calling and waiting for a nurse to unhook me and walk me to the bathroom, so a few days into my stay, the nurses put an alarm on my bed. Every time I got out of the bed, an alarm would sound. So I told Superia to lie in the bed to prevent the alarm from going off, then I would unplug all the wires and go to the bathroom. I was hooked up to everything imaginable, so even if I could get around with no assistance, all the machine hookups weren't going to let me go but so far. My vision was fuzzy: reading my phone messages was a true task. I couldn't write: I had minimum coordination with my hands. I remember finally finding my phone and trying to respond to overwhelming Facebook messages and text messages when I realized I couldn't do it. I couldn't direct my fingers to text. I spoke with a slur and had to take my time when responding to others to ensure they understood what I was saying. I am known for my fast talking, so this was a blow mentally for me.

Though the stroke caused quite a few effects, I didn't have any pain except on the second night in the hospital. I had the worst headache of my life; I literally cried and moaned most of the night because the pain was almost unbearable. The doctors and nurses tried a variety of different pain relievers, but none of them were giving me any relief. Superia, who sat in the chair next to me in tears, helplessly watched me as my dad prayed. The nurses advised me that my brain was swelling, a condition called cerebral edema. The swelling of my brain was causing pressure on my skull, and that was the reason for this horrible head pain.

After about forty-eight hours in the hospital, I had seen a total of eight different doctors: a hospitalist, a neurologist, a rheumatologist, a cardiologist, a hematologist oncologist, a physical therapist, an occupational therapist, and a speech therapist. I have never given so many vials of blood in my life. They toyed with various diagnoses, trying to find the reasons why I might have had the strokes. They considered pregnancy, drug use, cancer, lupus, heat stroke, heart issues, cholesterol blockage, and blood clotting disorders. They tested my blood for a range of disorders and diseases, and they even did genetic testing that had to be sent away. By day two in the hospital, they surgically implanted a loop device, which is a device that monitors your heart rhythm looking for any irregularities in your heartbeat. Irregularities in your heart rhythm can cause strokes as well. Along with all the blood tests, I had numerous CAT scans to look at my brain, MRIs to look at my blood vessels, and EKGs to look at my heart, but still no indication of a cause.

After a few more days passed, the doctors and hospital staff still had no idea why I'd had the strokes. This was concerning in itself, especially because they hadn't been small strokes and because I had had more than one. However, the time I spent in the hospital began a healing and restoration session between me and God.

Though I didn't have a diagnosis or know what was going on with me physically, that was only one aspect of what took place. I needed to start looking at the spiritual side of things. I know you are thinking, What's the spiritual side of a stroke? There isn't a spiritual side of a stroke, but God had allowed the stroke to happen, so I needed to start investigating what was going on spiritually. Anytime anything takes place in our lives, we should speak to God about it, as He is the answer to every question. I finally started replaying the past few months of my life in my head, trying to find a clue from God.

I started replaying dates and events that had taken place right before all of this had happened. I started this thought process on the day of my mom's sixtieth birthday. Her birthday, July 24, began to trigger my memory and cause me to reflect. My siblings, my mom's best friend, and I had planned a surprise birthday party for my mom prior to me having the strokes. My mom's best friend had to tell my mom after everyone got wind of my stroke because the party had to be cancelled and someone had to inform everyone who had been invited about the cancellation.

After several days, I finally began to get some alone time. My parents and daughter had remained at the hospital endlessly, and once they became comfortable with my progress and how alert I was, they started going home for periods of time to get some rest. My first real time alone, I started talking to God because I finally accepted the fact that I'd had a stroke. The quiet time was an opportunity to begin a real and honest conversation with God. My first impulse was to immediately begin questioning God. God, what did I do to deserve this? Why did you allow this to happen to me? I was trying to make sense of this situation, and I couldn't even begin to do that without answers.

chapter 8

Quiet Storm
(Physical Healing)

I spent a total of eight long days in the hospital doing physical therapy, occupational therapy, and speech therapy, trying to physically get better. The physical healing appeared to come naturally and improve day by day. The doctors constantly told me that having a stroke at thirty-eight years old worked in my favor because I was young and my body would heal at a much faster rate than an older person.

On Monday, July 29, 2019, I was released from Bayhealth Hospital. I wanted to go straight home, but Foster and my parents had other plans. We all agreed I would stay with my parents for a few days so they could monitor me. I stayed at my parents' house for a week and returned to my house the following Sunday. Foster was still hesitant about me going home. Since he was in Korea, he wanted to be sure someone would be able to monitor me. I reassured him that I would be fine, and Superia would be with me if anything happened. I was ready to get back into a routine; I needed to gain some kind of normality. That Monday, I got up and tried to move around a little because lying around caused this depressive mood. I had to get used to carefully going up and down the stairs in my house. I hadn't fully regained my balance yet. I lived in a three-story townhouse, and there were two flights of stairs between the entrance and my bedroom.

By the afternoon, I was starting to get hungry. My appetite had suffered while I was in the hospital. The stroke had caused issues with my stomach. Everything didn't agree with it, which caused me to lose about fifteen pounds. I went downstairs to heat up a cup of noodles. It was quick and didn't require me to stand for a long period of time. Standing for long periods caused me to feel dizzy and lose my balance at times. I finished eating my noodles and lay down for a nap. When I got up, I felt slightly disoriented. I got out of bed and went to use the bathroom. As soon as I finished in the bathroom and began to walk back into my room, I lost consciousness and hit the floor. I can remember thinking as I was falling, *Oh no, I am having another stroke.*

This time when I hit the ground, I immediately regained consciousness. I couldn't move, but I could hear everything going on around me. Superia and her best friend, Chloe, were next door in her room when they heard me hit the ground. I could hear Superia and Chloe rushing into my bedroom.

They moved quickly. I could hear Superia on the phone with my mom and then on the phone with 911.

On that day, August 5, 2019, I returned to Bayhealth Hospital by ambulance for what they initially diagnosed as syncope, which is the medical term for fainting or losing consciousness. Bayhealth later decided that the swelling from the strokes had caused a blood vessel to burst, and I had a small blood bleed, which they assured me was the reason for me losing consciousness. They checked to make sure I hadn't had another stroke. Thank God I hadn't. However, I now had blood on the brain. I had to remain in the hospital to be monitored. They also added a neurosurgeon to my long list of doctors. They informed me that the blood bleed on my brain had to be monitored to ensure that I wouldn't need surgery to stop the bleeding.

I spent four more days hospitalized. Two of those days were spent in the Intensive Care Unit. The doctors wanted to closely monitor the blood bleed, which could have been an indication of bigger problems. While hospitalized, during my second day, the doctors got the rest of the blood work back that they had initially done during my first stay. It was the last of my test results regarding my stroke, and everything came back normal. This meant I still had no explanation of why I'd had the strokes and now no definitive answers on the syncope episode that had ushered my return. Almost every doctor had a theory but nothing conclusive. They ran another round of tests on me during this stay at the hospital, and by the end of the four-day stay, my results were all in. Every single test came back normal.

One would think that every single test coming back normal would bring some sense of peace. It triggered the opposite effect. I returned home, and for the next two months, my mind was a battlefield. Anxiety and depression kicked in like I had never experienced before. I wrangled with so many toxic thoughts on a minute-to-minute basis. I had thoughts of dying every single day. I stopped getting out of bed. I wondered how I would get back to normal because I couldn't imagine living life in this condition. What was happening? My speech, walking, and writing were improving, but they were a constant reminder of what had taken place in my life. The fact that I had to concentrate when walking was enough to weigh on me, and the belt they used during physical therapy in case I lost my balance didn't make it any better. The fact that I still had blurry vision made walking into stores with glaring lights everywhere torture. I could not stay in the grocery store very long. It felt like a disco fever clip from a seventies movie. Lights appeared to be bright and spinning almost everywhere I looked. And since I still had a slur in my speech, I had to slow down and enunciate all of my words. I could barely write; my handwriting looked like a five-year-old's.

These were all constant reminders that made it impossible to be in denial of having a stroke. These effects forced me not only to accept that this had indeed happened, but they were a constant reminder of it. The physical effects began to weigh on my emotions. My mental health began to deteriorate. What added insult to injury was that I still didn't have any definitive explanation of why I'd had the strokes.

I tried to act normal when everyone was around, especially Superia. I honestly didn't want her worrying. She had field hockey camp, which she needed to be in attendance at, and I assured her I was fine. I wanted her to go back to her normal routine. I tried to mask the anxiety I was experiencing. I don't know if Superia bought it, but it was enough to convince her to go back to her normal routine. She played field hockey and lacrosse, and I didn't want her missing any conditioning because of me.

Meanwhile, Foster wasn't convinced. He would only call me with FaceTime at this point because he wanted to be able to see me and "read my spirit." He was definitely in tune with me and, more importantly, with God. He knew when I wasn't okay despite how much I tried to convince him otherwise. Foster was such a blessing during this difficult time. He kept reminding me to go back to the basics, to go back to what I knew worked as a Believer. He told me to go back to God.

I finally started praying more frequently. The prayers became so frequent, they turned into routine conversations. I started talking out loud to God. I needed to know He was hearing me. I told God I couldn't move on with my life having no answers. The next day, I decided I was going to get a second opinion. There was one problem—I needed my medical records to do so, and it seemed like such an over-whelming task for someone who still couldn't think clearly. How would I go about getting all those records when it took forever for me to even speak, let alone write? I didn't have the energy to go to the hospital to request them. I wasn't even sure where to begin.

God knows exactly what you need and when you need it. God's timing is perfect. The very next day, a longtime friend of mine, Dennis, who worked at the hospital, reached out to check on me. He had been checking in on me during my entire stays, both times, at the hospital. I told him my dilemma, and he came to my house so I could sign everything. Immediately, I got everything I needed to send off to get a second opinion. After submitting hundreds of pages of medical information, including medical records dating back to 2005, CT scans on CDs, EKG reports, and all my blood test results, I finally got an appointment at the Johns Hopkins Hospital's Neurology Department in Maryland. Johns Hopkins is number one in the nation for neurology. My appointment was scheduled for September 17, 2019, at 1:30 pm.

You would think that once I finally secured my appointment for a second opinion, I would finally have some level of peace. Nope, not at all. Again, it fostered quite the oppo-site effect. Instead, I began to elevate my toxic thoughts to a whole new level. I remember thinking, *These people are experts, number one in neurology in the country. What if they find some rare, crazy disease?*

My parents and I had a quiet and tense drive from Dover to Baltimore. It was the day after Superia's sixteenth birthday. I had tried to give her my full and undivided attention the day before, but all I could think about was that an appointment that could possibly decide my fate was scheduled for the following day.

After checking in and getting all the necessary paperwork completed, they called me back. My parents and I watched as the neurologist from Johns Hopkins pulled up my medical records from 2005 to the present on a big screen so we could all see them. As he pulled up each medical record, year by year, he analyzed every detail and finally concluded that there wasn't anything in the medical records that was abnormal except an abnormal Pap smear over ten years ago, seasonal allergies (hay fever), and a history of migraines. I began to feel a mix of relief and concern. I never really pondered the idea that the Johns Hopkins neurologist may not find anything either. He continued to explain how nothing in my medical history was concerning or a red flag. He also reviewed all the test results, one by one, from the thousands of blood tests taken by Bayhealth. He ruled out a variety of disorders and diseases. He concluded that he found no diseases and nothing remotely abnormal in any of the blood test results.

He finally asked me if I'd had a neck injury or had done something to my neck during that immediate period before having the strokes. He pulled up the MRI and MRA (magnetic resonance angiography) I had done while at Bayhealth. He showed me what he believed to be a vertebral artery dissection (VAD). I quickly began to scan the month of June 2019, and the light bulb lit up. I remembered an incident that had happened during that month. I had accidentally fallen asleep on my leather couch, which had sharp wooden arms. I would normally put a pillow on the arm because the arms were sharp. I was so tired, I fell asleep accidentally with no cushion or protection for my neck. The wooden arm dug into my neck because there was no cushion. The only reason I recalled this summer night was because I woke up early the next morning with the most excruciating neck pain. The pain was so bad I called my mom, complaining to her that I was in so much pain that I was thinking about going to the emergency room. Instead, I took two doses of acetaminophen and ibuprofen for several days until the pain became bearable and I could somewhat turn my neck.

The doctor explained that VAD is when there is a flap-like tear of the inner lining of the vertebral artery. After the tear, blood is able to enter the wall and begins to form a clot as it heals. So the body begins to heal itself, but the thickening causes clots that can impede blood flow. He explained how various things can cause this, from car accidents to sports injuries but sometimes with no explanation at all. He advised that, most of the time, the vessels heal themselves. He stated that these dissections rarely cause strokes; the percentage of them causing a stroke is very low. The problem arises when they go undetected because you lose out on getting the antiplatelet drugs such as aspirin to prevent them from clotting while healing. He reported that this was probably also the reason for all the clots in my brain. The tear went undetected and, therefore, untreated for so long, which allowed the clots to keep forming and then move through the blood flow in my brain. They moved around until the clots got big enough to obstruct blood flow, which caused the strokes. He specified that though it doesn't always cause strokes in young adults, when adults in their thirties have strokes, VAD is usually the cause. He explained how the Johns Hopkins Hospital had a remarkable stroke clinic and widely recognized stroke centers where they continued to gain knowledge from patients' pre- and post-stroke experiences along with cutting-edge research; they were stroke experts.

He ended my appointment by reassuring me that he believed VAD was the cause of my strokes. He hadn't uncovered any underlying conditions, disorders, or diseases, and this would most likely be the first and last time I would have to visit the Johns Hopkins Neurology Department for this incident. For the very first time in two months, I started to feel the weight being lifted. It was all beginning to make sense. Now I could breathe and return to normal because I had answers! Unfortunately, that didn't exactly happen.

chapter 9

Mental Healing–
Spiritual Respiration

Going to Johns Hopkins and getting some concrete information that allowed for an explanation and even a diagnosis only relieved me from the physical defects in my body from the stroke. That alone was a great start to being able to get back to some kind of normality. I started to play with the idea of going back to work. The doctor's report from Johns Hopkins gave me some peace about what had medically taken place to cause the strokes. Nonetheless, it was only one piece to the puzzle. God had allowed this to happen. I started to think about how the spiritual aspect of this incident needed to be addressed. God doesn't do anything by coincidence. Everything that happens in life happens for a reason.

I had to first remind myself that God loved me and wouldn't do anything to hurt me. He may have allowed stuff to happen to make me uncomfortable, but it was always for a purpose. I needed to accept that fact. And instead of complaining and being angry, I needed to spend time with God so I could get instruction and understanding on what God wanted me to learn, know, and/or do. We can never really know for sure the "why" in everything we experience on this earth. There are times in our life when things happen or take place because we caused them. If you are driving above the speed limit, there is a chance you could get pulled over and get a ticket. Those types of things are natural consequences to natural actions.

Then there are times when things happen that we don't cause or are beyond our control. We go to the doctor's office and get a bad diagnosis or a bad report. When things take place in our life that we didn't cause, understanding why becomes a bit more complex to figure out and even harder to accept. Sometimes it's because God is trying to get our attention or teach us something. If God is allowing a situation to help us gain strength, trust Him, or acquire patience, it's for a reason.

There are also times when we go through things for other people. God is trying to teach something or get the attention of someone around us or connected to us but chooses to use us to do it. Maybe God wants to get a point across to your family member or even a friend, but He desires to use you because there's a connection and it will be more effective. Sometimes we go through things, and we have absolutely no clue why. Those are probably the most difficult to digest because we know God loves us, but it's hard to wholeheart-edly believe that when you are in pain, angry, frustrated, hurt, experiencing lack, or trying to accept a serious medical diagnosis or recover from a medical emergency.

One thing I can attest to is that trying to understand the purpose for my incident was difficult. I had to stop looking at it from the perspective of "Why is God trying to hurt me?" but instead start saying, "God, what are you trying to tell me? What do you want me to get out of this? You needed to get my attention because you allowed this to take place. I repent and am sorry if I ignored various other signs prior to this hap-pening, but I am listening now!" Seeking answers from God caused me to go deeper in prayer, learn to meditate and listen for His voice, and get to know Him even better by constantly reading His Word. Through this process, I was able to rebuild my relationship with God, and God began to give me so much revelation surrounding my strokes.

I finally began to heal mentally. I knew that in order to con-tinue to heal mentally, I needed more familiarity and more routine. I started back to work on October 7, 2019. Getting back into a work routine definitely helped even more with my mental state. This was an opportunity for me to begin to get acclimated to the new position I had never started because I'd had the stroke right before the school year had started. All of these things helped me get back into my normal routine, but nighttime was still a struggle. I still had to work on the toxic and negative thoughts I was having.

I began working hard on my deliverance. "Deliverance" is a term Believers use when they are trying to get free from something or be liberated from bondage or ungodly strongholds. I needed deliverance from this detrimental mindset I had built after my stroke. During the past few months, I felt like I was completely losing the mental battle. It was a fight for me to maintain sanity immediately after my strokes. I created a mindset I didn't even recognize. I have never been a fearful or anxious person, but at one point, that was all I knew. I ultimately needed deliverance from myself. My mental state caused my faith to deteriorate, and I became my own biggest enemy. However, deep down in the crevices of my heart, underneath everything I had allowed to take root after my stroke, I was reminded that I had a real relationship with God. I knew the God I served, and that mustard seed of faith was what finally began to activate. Every day I told myself God loved me, and I asked Him what He wanted me to learn in all of this. I knew He had allowed me to have the strokes because He was trying to get something out of me.

This was where the battle got intense. I returned to praying every day and building my inner man because I refused to let the flesh or carnal (human) part of me rule any longer. I could literally hear the battle raging in my mind most days. I kept allowing my mind to tell me that God couldn't love me and allow this to take place in my life. My mind kept telling me that God was punishing me. I started recalling the morning of my stroke: how God had told me to go to church, and I had responded with "I'm not going to church. I hate church." Why had I become so rebellious? Maybe God had had enough of me. I needed God to talk to me. I continued to petition Him daily in prayer. I stayed on my knees, not so much for answers from Him, but asking Him for forgiveness for going astray. I kept praying that God would change my perspective and how I was looking at the entire experience. I asked God to show me me. I thanked Him over and over, on a daily basis, for allowing me to live.

I stayed in a constant posture of prayer. I needed to renew my mind in Jesus to get rid of these toxic thoughts. The enemy was busy and was sending me more wicked thoughts than I could keep up with. I knew these were thoughts from the enemy because they were thoughts I would have never even entertained prior to my stroke. I thought about dying daily; I would think up reasons why God might take me out. Every once in a while the enemy would throw a suicidal thought in. It got to a point where the thoughts became so crippling to me, I started to isolate myself. When family and friends called, I would assure them I was just fine. I would sit on the phone for a few minutes to play the role of fine and then hang up and return to my depression/anxiety state, which usually took place in bed. I talked to Foster every single night. He stayed on the phone with me, the majority of the time praying for me as I lay there, so I would be able to fall asleep.

I remember one night after struggling to fall asleep that I woke up because I felt a presence in my bedroom. I looked toward the doorway to see if Superia might be standing there. She wasn't awake. I could hear her grinding her teeth while sleeping as she has done since she was a small child. As I continued to stare at the doorway of my bedroom, I watched the outline of a spirit appear.

I know you are thinking, Now hold on, this isn't a horror book. Nope, it's not, but it's an account of exactly what happened. There was a demon standing at the doorway of my bedroom. I know that sounds far-fetched, spooky, and crazy. I know you are wondering how I knew it was a demon. I can't explain how I knew, I just knew it wasn't anything of God. What had just walked into my bedroom was evil. Its blurred face and outline screamed wicked. The demon walked right into my bedroom and sat at the foot of my bed on the left side. I remember freezing in place and just watching him.

He uttered quietly but as clear as day, "I hope you know you are going to die."

Instead of being intimidated and absolutely terrified, I instantly became furious. This was the last straw; this was my breaking point. At that very moment, I decided I had let the enemy run amuck and fill a vacancy in my mind for way too long.

"I am sick of you!" were my exact words. I immediately started calling on Jesus. I yelled His name over and over. I began to pray with my eyes closed, and when I opened them, the demon was gone. This marked the beginning of my deliverance.

After four months of dealing with the battle in my mind,

it finally came to an end. In December 2019, I had my last memorable fight with this crippling anxiety and depression. It had been going on for four consecutive months since my stroke. Going back to work, going back to church, and doing normal things around the house allowed me to finally return to some kind of normality, but there was still this lingering feeling of anxiousness.

It was Sunday, and since I was back to my normal routine, I had gotten dressed for church. I sat toward the back, as I felt more comfortable near the back where I could hear the word but not have to socialize with too many people just yet. I was sitting right in a pew of my church, and the enemy began to speak to me so loud and clear. "Don't even think you are out of the woods. You have an even higher chance of having a second stroke once you have had one. You could have one right here in this church. There's no power in here."

I'd never really understood or experienced anxiety until after the strokes, and at times it became unbearable and uncontrollable to a point that sometimes it would cause panic attacks. I had learned through my own experience how anxiety worked. It had become second nature to me. My mind would first set off signs, triggers, and warnings that would then translate physically to my body. It's the craziest feeling I have ever experienced, mainly because it's a feeling that is almost impossible to control. It reminds me of how superheroes mutate when they change from the normal person to the creature with the superpowers (except you don't get any superpowers!).

Once my mind convinced me that I needed to be on guard (despite not being in any clear or present danger), I would "transform," for lack of a better word. My body started to increase my heart rate, my breathing began to change, and I began to go into fight-or-flight mode because that's how your body physically responds when it believes there is a threat. So right when I was about to flee, take my exit out of the church, I looked down at my phone and texted Foster.

Foster had become my first point of contact for just about everything in my life: good, bad, and ugly. No, he wasn't perfect, and neither was I, but we were perfect for each other. The crazy part is that we went to high school together. He was in a grade level above me, but we never really crossed paths. Foster often speaks about this one memory he has of me. He recalls seeing me walking down the library hallway of Dover High School, the school we attended and the high school Superia currently attends. I was in the hallway cursing. He says he thought, "Skinny Minnie is always cursing."

We have a great bond, and it is because God was the foundation of it. He is finally the man I can rely on. And ever since my stroke, I've begun to rely on him even more. He knows it. He continued to be my support thousands of miles away, at any hour of the day, but he always gave me God. He reminded me that he loved making sure I was good, but always reiterated he wasn't God.

In the text, I told him what was going on and how I was about to get up and basically run out of the church. He quickly responded no. He persuaded me to stay there in church. He stated he was about to start praying. The crazy part was that I almost responded, "What's that going to do?" I almost didn't trust the prayers I so freely suggested to everyone else as solutions when they expressed they had a problem. Life has a way of showing the Believer where they honestly are in their walk with Christ. Nonetheless, I decided I would give him about sixty seconds to send these prayers. After fifty-nine seconds, my tense body began to relax. I stopped sweating, and I immediately started crying. He texted me repeatedly, making sure I had stayed and was okay. His exact words were "Queen, God has you, and so do I." Needless to say, the anxiety subsided, and I was able to remain at church until the end. The peace that came over me that day in church I knew was no longer temporary or just for that moment. The mental exhaustion I had experienced for the past few months was definitely due to my traumatic stroke experience. However, it was intensified due to my weakened spiritual state. But that day as I cried in the pew at church, I knew it was finally over. It was evident that my mental healing was tied to my spiritual state. It was at this moment I begin to feel a new spiritual strength. I knew God was about to give me a second wind. I was exhausted, but God was about to renew my mind and my spirit in Him, as that was the only thing that could give me rest. He was about to give me the ability to breathe again, spiritually, which I can best describe as spiritual respiration.

• chapter 10 •

Restoring My Faith/ Turning Around for Me

The twenty-first of July was a constant reminder of one of the scariest days of my life; it was the day I could have lost my life if it wasn't for God's grace and mercy. I considered the date a bittersweet commemoration, as it served as a reminder of the event, but in the same breath, every time I made it to the twenty-first of a month, it also served as a reminder that God had allowed me to live another month. My mom often said, "God works in mysterious ways." This is not a Scripture; however, there were so many instances in my life I could see how the saying might be true.

Anyway, I was downstairs in my classroom overseeing the recovery intervention for failing students. Since I wasn't able to start the school year off in August, as I was still recuperating then, I wasn't able to implement the plan I'd worked so hard on during most of the summer. My boss was just happy to see me in a good state of health and back to work. So I had just jumped in when I got back to work and did anything that needed to be done to help struggling students. I was responsible for instructing five sections of students who had failed a content area the previous marking period and were working on recouping the skills to recover the grade. On the twenty-first of November, 2019, the front office called my classroom. The front office lady, whom I considered another mom, informed me that district leadership (superintendents) was in the building and was requesting to speak to me.

Completely caught off guard, I became instantly curious. I briefly reviewed the past few weeks in my mind to make sure I hadn't done anything crazier than normal. I couldn't think of anything, plus I hadn't been back to work two months, so I couldn't have done anything too crazy yet. I considered myself a true advocate for my students. I was continually speaking on their behalf regarding instruction and pedagogy on any platform that allowed space for me to do so.

Therefore, I couldn't think of the slightest reason for why the superintendents desired to speak to me; I had no idea what this impromptu meeting was about. To make a long story short, the alternative school in our district was in need of a leader, as their leader had taken a leave of absence. They decided to temporarily pull the eighth-grade principal from our middle school, as she had prior experience as a head principal, to lead the alternative school. They approached my building principal with the proposal to take over as eighth-grade principal, but stated they would need someone, such as a teacher leader, to take on the assistant principal role while she fulfilled her special assignment. They all agreed that I was the person for the job.

After only six weeks of being back at school and working in my new position as RTI coordinator, I was now placed in the position as the interim, or acting, assistant principal at CMS for an indefinite period of time. This was probably the first time out of the thirty-eight years of my life that I couldn't think of a word to say.

"Out of the few years I have known you, this is probably the first time I have seen you with nothing to say" were the exact words spoken by one of the superintendents.

I walked out of the meeting in complete shock. I immediately went back to my classroom where I was met by a group of students who were lined up outside of the class, waiting on me. I could barely focus enough to get the students started on the intervention. The work for the intervention was online, so each student did their work on computers. I was still trying to process my news. I was trying to grasp what my new position was going to entail. When I finally got to my planning period, I went out to my car and cried my eyes out.

"Wow. God" was the only thing I kept saying over and over to myself. Here it was, the twenty-first of the month, and I was getting a promotion on the same date I'd had my stroke. My first phone call was, of course, to my love, Foster. I had texted him earlier to tell him I had some big news to share. I called him and couldn't get it out fast enough. The excitement in his voice was just more validation that I had picked the right man. He was most definitely "my person," and the past four months had provided more evidence and proof that God had picked him for me. I then called my dad and mom to tell them the good news, and both were ecstatic to hear good news from me. Having the strokes had really taken a toll on my entire family. We were close, and we hated to see any of us suffering.

I worked for six months as the interim assistant principal for Central Middle School. I was pulled into a leadership position with no warning or administration experience while still trying to physically and mentally heal. I wasn't sure I was even ready for a task of this caliber. Nevertheless, the Book of Psalms in the Bible tells us that promotion, advancement, and elevation don't come from man but from God. And when God calls you to do anything, He will most definitely equip you to do it. That's exactly what He did for me. He equipped me to do the job.

Unfortunately, not everyone considered my news good. Not even thirty days into my new role, I was already experiencing resistance from staff. If it wasn't a complaint to my principal, it was a complaint to the district office. I remember thinking that I should go to my principal and the superintendents to tell them they needed to find someone else to do this job. I was, in the most humble way, trying to make things better. I was trying to incorporate things to get everyone on the same page.

This was a true flashback to when I'd gotten Teacher of the Year in 2017. So many teachers were upset about an award they had said didn't mean anything and was solely a popularity contest. In order to get Teacher of the Year, you had to be a teacher for at least three years and be tenured to get the award. They called Human Resources to make sure I had my three years as a classroom teacher. They started so many rumors that year in regard to the award. They made up stories, such as my principal stuffed the ballot box for me, the count was wrong, and I shouldn't have won. They complained that the process needed to be changed and should include the community and parents.

The funny thing is, two years later, they did change the Teacher of the Year process. However, I was nominated every year even with the new process, which included being nominated by members of the community. The new process actually brought even more nominations as well as a message on why I should be picked. I took my name off the list every year after I won in 2017. I didn't want to go through that hoopla again, and I didn't need any award to attest to the fact that I was an amazing teacher. My students were living proof.

Anyhow, I started getting emotional about this new role. Anything I did to better our processes or procedures at CMS was met with some kind of opposition. I was reminded in this position that anytime God calls you to an assignment for His purpose, the enemy is always waiting to sabotage the plan. It was my job to ensure that the enemy didn't gain any more space in my head, as I had finally gotten to a way better place mentally.

In this interim assistant principal position, I gained invaluable insight about leadership. There were three principal themes that stood out. The most crucial one was to understand that, being a leader in any setting, you must recognize that you are first a servant. This first theme immediately reminded me of Jesus. Jesus's entire ministry was based on serving. You cannot correctly lead if you have never served. The second theme was in order to be an effective leader, you must be an effective listener. When you are trying to improve or change things for the better, you need to hear what your people are saying as well as what your people are not saying. This is not the time to be defensive or make excuses. The last theme was solidified in John C. Maxwell's 21 Most Powerful Minutes in a Leader's Day. He states, "The more leadership ability a person has, the more quickly he recognizes leadership—or its lack—in others" (Thomas Nelson 2000, 99). The more I learned what leadership looked like, the more I realized that there were a lot of people in positions of authority surrounding me who weren't necessarily leaders. I didn't just learn important leadership styles and strategies in this role, but I was reminded of the importance of accountability, the power of influence, and how humility is necessary to continue to progress and grow as a leader. I had the opportunity to sit alongside some amazing administrators who worked tirelessly and continued to level up even through a pandemic. No amount of schooling and/or professional development could have prepared me for what I was blessed to experience in this role at such an uncanny time. Being in an administrative role allowed me to see a different perspective. I was finally able to see the big picture in the district, not just the parts at the teacher level. This simply reaffirmed the concerns that I had already identified throughout my career: the educational system needed a change.

On June 30, 2020, my special role as interim associate principal ended. I returned to the role of RTI coordinator with a wealth of knowledge. Little did I know, God was just getting started with the restoration in my life through grace, mercy, and favor.

• chapter 11 •

Blessings upon Blessings

Superia, being my one and only biological child, had endured a lot by this point in her life. Her resilience grew while being raised by a single mother, and she exhibited extreme endurance through my recovery process. I was more of a disciplinarian than a nurturer. I kept the standards and expectations high for her while providing her as much support as I possibly could. Whether it was emotional support, spiritual support, or monetary support, I made sure it happened. I wanted her to be able to reach each and every goal she set out to do. I didn't want her to ever have any excuse as to why she couldn't. My prayer for Superia was that she would keep God first, remain humble in everything she did, and achieve her dreams.

On September 1, 2020, God definitely answered one of

my prayers in regard to Superia. God opened doors only He could open by giving Superia a platform to showcase her gift and be able to achieve one of her dreams.

Superia was going into her sophomore year of high school when I had my stroke. During the 2020–2021 school year, she was a junior at Dover High in Capital School District, the district I also worked in. Unfortunately, since I worked for Capital School District, she was always in the limelight. Superia was always "Ms. Smith's daughter," which was never truly in her favor. The only benefit for that type of attention was that the students I taught were like my family. Therefore, when she got to high school, the students I had taught were there, so she already had a family ready to look out for her. During Superia's first days at the high school, she would come home daily to tell me that numerous students had approached her to ask if she was my daughter, to introduce themselves, and to let her know that if she needed anything, they were around.

In June 2019, Superia went to school with me during the summer while I was preparing for my RTI coordinator position. Superia has had a top-ten colleges list since middle school. I instructed her to get all the pertinent information about admissions for the universities that she had on her list. I then made her send emails introducing herself to these colleges with a few sports clips of her playing field hockey and lacrosse. These were simply videos that I had on my phone. I also instructed her to send her sports schedule for the school she played for. No responses came from any of them.

About a month after my stroke, I made her go back and reach out again, just trying to get her attention focused on school and away from my traumatic stroke experience. She gave me resistance, saying that no one was going to respond. I reminded her that when something is God's will, it will come to pass. God's will will be done, but "faith without works is dead" (James 2:26). In other words, just believing in God wasn't going to cut it. She had to put in the work.

At this time, Superia played for a travel team, Eastern Shore Lacrosse Club (ESLC). This travel team was stationed in southern Delaware. When Chloe's dad, Dante, had brought this team to my attention, I hadn't thought twice when I'd said no. I'd had enough on my plate with her being a scholar and an athlete. I was always on the go. All I could think about was that if I allowed her to join one more thing, it would mean more money, more time, and a bunch of traveling. Anyone who knows me knows I hate driving, and this team had tournaments on weekends in various states to play other club teams.

Dante and his wife, Tyra, along with Chloe, Superia's best friend, were attending the same church as us at the time, and I will never forget this particular Sunday. Right in church, Dante pulled out the waiver for Superia to try out for the team. I guess he figured I couldn't say no while in the house of the Lord. I remember his words that day to me: "I have a plan, sis. Trust me." Needless to say, I signed the waiver, and Superia, Chloe, and Dante darted out of church at the end of service to go to these tryouts. The rest is history!

Superia, one of the few African American players, along with Chloe, not only made the team, but was welcomed with open arms. The players and parents of ESLC became another family to us. I watched this club mold my daughter in skills, speed, and her IQ of the game. Superia had no choice but to improve her game and get to their level while playing with this team. Superia played with girls who had been playing lacrosse since they were a very young age. A lot of times, when others referred to these girls from Cape and lacrosse, they would say "someone put a stick in their hand when they first started walking." In other words, these girls were super-stars at lacrosse. Superia hadn't started playing lacrosse until middle school, but what helped her was that she was athletic.

Athleticism appeared to be genetic. My sister, Tyresa, had played professional basketball in her time and had even been drafted as the eighteenth overall pick in the 2007 WNBA draft. My father had been a great baseball player in his day, showing us newspaper articles showcasing his talent. He pulled them out every once in a while when a family member made it into the newspaper for their highlights of a game.

Superia's athleticism allowed her to not only play field hockey and lacrosse, but to become quite remarkable in both sports. I loved watching her play lacrosse. My mom had given her the nickname Baked Bean when she was young because of her golden brown skin. I loved watching my little Baked Bean take the field. In both sports, her speed on the field was unmatched.

In the summer of 2020, God gave Superia a platform on which to be seen. God allowed divine opportunity for Superia: she was at the right place at the right time for the right people to see her play lacrosse. September 1, 2020, was the first day Division 1 schools could reach out to an athlete to show their interest for a student entering into their junior year. Boy, did we wake up to unexpected emails and text messages. Superia received messages from various Division 1 colleges, including Ivy League schools.

In the past few years, anytime someone requested Superia's college list or even asked where my daughter desired to go, they never knew how to react to the list I gave them. They would usually say something along the lines of the fact that those colleges were pretty hard to get into. I would think to myself, *Well, obviously, and what's your point?* My daughter was not just capable of going Division 1 as an athlete, but she was also capable as a scholar. So many coaches told me that she would only get certain looks from certain colleges, but those top schools probably weren't going to be an option.

There are three crucial things I learned through this experience and being the parent of an athlete: (1) Don't let anyone tell you or your child that they can't or that something is unattainable or impossible. Our children have enough barriers to contend with in their generation. Don't let others put limitations on your child. Yes, they need reality, but always set the bar high. God ultimately has the final say in every situation. (2) You are your child's first coach. There are many things coaches do regarding their players that I don't always agree with, but I make sure I'm the primary person feeding my daughter what she needs both mentally and spiritually. I put in her spirit what needs to be put in and take out what doesn't belong there. Simple as that. (3) I am a firm believer that you reap what you sow. As an educator, I have always taken care of everyone else's children to the best of my ability. I have given and sacrificed for so many children I didn't birth, and in return, God definitely took care of mine.

It was incredible to speak to many prestigious colleges and hear them not just talk about all the amazing qualities they saw in Superia on the field or on film, but they also raved about how she was a true student athlete after looking over her transcripts. They spoke about how impressive it was that she kept over a 4.0 GPA while carrying a load of AP classes and playing two school sports as well as club teams. Despite how highly they spoke about her skills on the field and her grades, they seemed most impressed with how polite, humble, and well-mannered Superia was once they spoke to her. At one point, the women's lacrosse coach from Princeton said, "You have obviously done a great job as a parent." After weighing all factors, Superia verbally committed to a Division 1 college for lacrosse.

On September 20, 2020, when Superia made her final decision on which college to commit to, it was another reminder of how faithful God is. The hardships, trials, and tribulations I worked through in my seventeen years as a single mother were not in vain. God was with me along the way, preparing for this very day. What remained true was that, as long as I put my confidence in God, He will never fail me. God was showing me that despite how, at times, I was faithless, He will always remain faithful to who He is. I needed to learn to stop talking so much and do more listening to God.

For some reason we tend to trust God with certain areas of our life, but not all areas. It's not until we trust God with everything that we will be able to witness God's true sovereignty. I trusted Him with my healing both physically and mentally after the strokes, and God kept His promise. I trusted God with my daughter's next steps and future regarding college, and He kept His promise. God has a remarkable track record, and it is evident that trusting Him is a win-win situation.

But I needed to give up one last area I continued to hold on to and tried to be in control of. It was time to relinquish control of the final area: my intimate relationships. Did I trust God to bring me my husband?

chapter 12

Trusting God with Everything

After experiencing such a traumatic experience with my stroke, God had me reassess so many areas of my life. I kept trying to keep the relationship area out, but God wouldn't allow me to. Who did God desire me to spend my life with? My past track record with relationships proved I had not done the best job of choosing a partner. I don't know why it was difficult to trust God with this, as He had provided and taken care of me the entire time I was a single parent. Better yet, God had provided for me my entire life, and even more recently had shown His loving kindness with my recovery during my stroke.

Though my dad was a pastor and the scholar of God's Word, when I was growing up, it was my mom who continued to encourage me to petition God for myself. She would always remind me to say grace, say my prayers, and thank God for everything. She was always in a constant posture of prayer.

Listening to various conversations, it was easy to tell she was humble in spirit when it came to God. She was not perfect but had a reverence for God.

"Terry, you coming to Maryland?" Her response to any invite she accepted was "God willing." She always reminded me that God was in control. Though my desire to learn and study God's Word was influenced by my father, my mother was who I drew my strength from. She was an amazing mother, always sacrificing for her children. She had old-school morals and values. When I told my parents I was pregnant, it took both of my parents by surprise. They'd been married when they'd had me, my brother, and my sister. Therefore, when I had my single-parent issues, they honestly couldn't weigh in. Being a single parent came with circumstances they had no knowledge or experience with, and therefore, my relationship with God was even more necessary.

There's something about being a single parent that forces you to "take it on the chin" or "man up," for a lack of better words. As a single mother, I had the tendency to build an internal wall and a tough exterior for protection. When you hear the word "protection," you immediately think physical protection, but protection from physical encounters isn't what I'm speaking about. I refused to repeat the past hurts and disappointments. I needed to protect my feelings; I needed protection for my heart. Independence was one of the ways I did just that. I know that sounds weird; how can independence be used as protection?

Easy. If I set my life up in a way where I relied only on myself to do everything, which meant I didn't ask anyone for anything, I couldn't possibly be disappointed. Now, I didn't say it was the smartest way to protect my feelings or the smartest way to protect my heart, but it definitely worked. When you have been independent for so long, becoming vulnerable and learning to trust and become dependent on another person can be a challenging task. Sometimes in a relationship this never takes place. However, if it's going to happen at all, it's going to take time and patience. It doesn't happen overnight.

Not only was I not used to relying on anyone, but I was not used to anyone taking the lead in my life. I had always been the head of the house as a single mother; the only people in my life who were consistent and reliable were my parents and siblings. But then God sent me Foster, a man who did things without being asked, who loved me unconditionally, and who always made sure I was mentally and spiritually well. All of this definitely took some getting used to, but I finally accepted it. I accepted Foster's help and recognized that God had handpicked him for me.

Most of the time after a few relationships, especially bad ones, we are convinced we know what we need and what we want in a mate. Yet we can still be totally wrong. The problem is, in our past relationships, we have become so accustomed to dysfunction that we view it as normal. We make dysfunction normal and, unfortunately, use it as criterion for our future relationships. Consequently, when we enter into the next relationship with a different person and they have different bad habits, characteristics, and traits but still offer the same toxicity, we accept it. We compare the new toxicity to the previous toxicity and decide we are in a better predicament because they aren't exactly the same. Ultimately, we believe we are in a better relationship when, in all reality, we are not. We have simply swapped the old set of problems for a new set of problems. This harmful behavior can give us a false perception of what is healthy as well as what is normal. This false perception also leads us to believe other myths and lies, such as when we experience rough times with certain people, we need to remain in the toxicity simply because we have shared some obstacles in this toxic relationship. This mindset will have you telling yourself, "We (you and your partner) can't give up because we have been through too much together." Then there is the other end of the spectrum: the mindset that since we have experienced suffering in our past relationships, we deserve to have someone come and save us. We feel like we deserve more than a relationship because we desire a savior. We have unrealistic expectations for that person to be absolutely perfect. Neither of these concepts is accurate, logical, or healthy.

What I have learned from being in a healthy relationship with Foster is that in order to be a part of a healthy relationship, you first must be healthy and/or whole. Before entering into a relationship, you must first clean up your own act. In an intimate relationship, we have a habit of carrying our baggage with us and unloading it at each stop (in each relationship) instead of sorting through it (processing what we have been through) and discarding the junk. We don't need to enter into any relationship until we deal with our own issues. That doesn't mean you have to be perfect or free of all residue of your mess, but you must acknowledge what your issues are and know what needs to be done to rectify them. The reality is that if you aren't content or have peace with yourself, you will never be able to find it in another person. Only God has the ability to do that.

I had one essential stipulation for whomever I ended up with: the number one requirement was that he had to be a God-fearing man. I wasn't interested in just a churchgoer, because there are plenty of devils who attend church, but a man who wholeheartedly loved God. Foster absolutely loves God, so he is inevitably honest, genuinely caring, and a giver. He is patient with me. I'm not the easiest person to deal with, but he also knows when to draw the line when he's had enough attitude from me. Foster knows how and when to hold me accountable. He has no problem calling me out on my mess, but from a loving place. He pushes me in areas I am weak. He is supportive and has my back in all of my many endeavors, from my small business (my non-profit organization) to my ministry with students. He makes sure I lack nothing in my household. He takes care of my daughter like she is his own. Most importantly, he makes sure I lack nothing spiritually, and because of that, I realize he is my future.

To be honest, I was never sure about marriage being in my future. I felt the same way about having kids, didn't want any, but miraculously I still managed to have one. What I did decide early on in life was that if I ever decided to get married, it would probably be pretty fairy-tale-ish. Unfortunately, like most females, any serious thoughts on a union probably revolved around a fairy-tale wedding instead of focusing on a fairy-tale marriage.

I was blessed to witness a genuine union between my parents, but I didn't always admire my parents' relationship until I had matured. As time passed and I got older, my respect for my parents' marriage grew more and more. My parents didn't have the perfect marriage, but God knows what they had was solid and real. I watched them for forty years take care of each other, even at the lowest point of each of their lives. I watched my mom take care of my dad after a major surgery when they removed a majority of his intestines and he had a colostomy bag for a short period of time. And I watched my dad take care of my mom as she fought and won her battle against cancer.

Continuing to watch them as the years passed began to give me a great perspective on what a "real" marriage could withstand with God as a part of the equation. God, love, honor, sacrifice, and compromise were all factors that were evident in my parents' relationship. Those are crucial characteristics in a great relationship, and they were what I began to recognize in my relationship with Foster.

chapter 13

God's Union

Foster had been in Korea for barely a few weeks when I'd had my stroke. Despite the thousands of miles between us, he was a crucial factor in my recovery. His encouraging spirit, constant prayers, and relentless reminders of God's promises to us were a big factor in me keeping my sanity and overall ability to keep my mental state together during such a rough period. His strong and unshakeable faith helped spark and put a fire back in my faith. His faith helped renew my mind in Jesus and helped me rebuild my faith little by little every single day. He told me every day that I was whole, I was healed, and God would restore me.

Foster and I had been getting to know each other since 2017. As time passed and we began to grow closer and more serious in our relationship, I began to worry. I started to raise concerns about our long-distance relationship. I began to wonder how we were going to do this. I would rehearse scenarios in my head constantly. Would I leave my family and my career and pack up Superia to move to Texas where he was stationed? Or would I have to wait out his active duty time until he retired? He had always talked about returning to his hometown in Delaware after he retired. We as Believers often think we have to figure out every little detail of our life when, in reality, we serve a sovereign God. God doesn't need our help. We forget that we serve His purpose and we don't need to figure out a plan, but instead we simply need to learn to yield to God's perfect plan that He has already purposed for our life.

Right before Foster had left for Korea, they had sent down orders for him to be stationed in Fort Dix in New Jersey, which was only approximately eighty miles from my house. God knew exactly what He was doing. So, when he returned from Korea back to the States, and after two different delays because of COVID-19, Foster officially reported to the East Coast on September 1, 2020. Elated doesn't describe how excited I was for us to finally shift our long-distance relationship to an in-person relationship. We had managed to have a strong and worthwhile long-distance relationship since we had made an official commitment in March of 2018. Foster had already served close to twenty years in the United States Army when we started dating.

In his army life, he had been to war and well over forty countries. I wasn't sure how I would fare as a military spouse. He had been to Germany, Kuwait, and Korea in the short time we had been together. Though I was only experiencing mild ramifications of this military life, it was already a struggle for me. I wasn't used to the distance, the not knowing what was next, the constant changes, and the nonstop uneasy feeling every time he was not in the country. Right around the time when I felt like I wouldn't be able to cope any longer with the distance, the news of his move to Fort Dix came down the pike. God's timing was perfect.

When he finally got here, he began to get settled in New Jersey, moving all his belongings onto post, or his duty station. He spent most of his time in Delaware with me and his family.

I have a vivid memory of a few days before my stroke where we had a serious conversation about our future. He told me all the reasons he knew I was his wife. Foster is a man of few words. Once we started dating, one thing I learned immediately about him was that he doesn't say things he doesn't mean. In our relationship, I watched him come out of a guarded place. He watched and listened to everything I said and did. This was all new to me. In my previous relationships, I was used to saying things I didn't mean sometimes to get the other person's attention. If you hurt me or upset me, I would, in return, say things to hurt you, even if I didn't mean them. I realized early on with Foster that I couldn't operate like this. I'd better say what I meant and mean what I said because he was going to take it for face value.

Anyway, the conversation we had before my stroke was a serious one. He talked about all of my qualities and the great characteristics I had as a person. He expressed all of the reasons he loved me. He expressed how much he appreciated me and truly valued me. I was so speechless, I didn't really respond, maybe because I didn't know how to. I had never had someone genuinely love me and celebrate me the way he did. I continued to just listen to what he had to say. So, the week I had my stroke and was in the hospital, that conversation was one of the first conversations that came to my remembrance. It almost came back in slow motion. I am not sure why, maybe because the stroke had me processing things at a slower pace, but what stood out to me was that, after our conversation, I hadn't really responded to him. One of the first things I said to him when I became cognizant in the hospital was that I did want to marry him. It's crazy how the brain works. His words were one of the first things that came to my mind as I began healing, and I wanted him to know at that very moment that I felt the same so he didn't have a doubt in his mind. I wanted him to know that the love was reciprocated.

As soon as he got to New Jersey, we discussed and immediately got moving on our goals and future plans. After three weeks passed, on a Sunday after church, Foster and I had one of the deepest conversations we have ever had about everything in our life. Soon after the conversation, he presented me with an engagement ring. We had already set our wedding date and had started making plans even before he got to New Jersey, so this was more of a formality, but it didn't change the feeling of excitement. I was still excited about the declaration he was making by presenting me with a ring. That night, as I took the ring off to place it in the box for the night, God began to speak to me at that very moment.

"Daughter, I realize you want to celebrate. I know you want to brag about your beautiful ring and talk to everyone about what dress you plan to wear on your wedding day, but there's something so much bigger taking place right now that I need you to understand." God reminded me that it wasn't about how in love I was (and I was definitely in love) or about how he was my best friend or how he had proved to be an amazing support during one of the lowest points of my life. All of that was crucial in ensuring that he was the right one, but those things weren't what God wanted me to focus on.

This union was going to be about God's assignment and purpose for our lives. God revealed to me that not only did we both have individual purposes in God, but we also had a purpose together. God expressed that this wasn't the time to relax or get too preoccupied with surface and/or material things. It was the time to seek Him even more.

A few days after this incredible moment, we acknowledged God's push to do what was right. God reminded us that so many people were watching us and that we needed to be an example of how, even in today's world, it is still right to do right. With that being said, we couldn't be under the same roof the majority of the time gambling with sin. We had already set a wedding date, but it was months away. God's requirements are for everyone. No one is exempt; therefore, we had a decision to make. Too often we think that because we desire to do right, God will excuse us. That's not how it works. The desire to do right is not enough. We have to do right. God honors our actions. We were adamant about doing things the right way. We wanted God to orchestrate this plan because it truly wasn't about us. It was about God's will for our life.

On October 1, 2020, I married my best friend at the Kent County Clerk of the Peace office. We set our formal wedding date for our one-year anniversary. It was the best decision we could have made together.

chapter 14

God's Purpose for My Life

*A*ll the trials and tribulations in my lifetime have contributed to molding who I am, but having a stroke was a life-changing event. When life honestly begins to happen, all the great godly advice we as Believers so freely give means nothing unless it is actually applied. I am constantly encouraging others to have faith. You lose a house or car, have faith. A relationship goes bad, have faith. You don't know how you are going to pay your bills, have faith. "Have faith" is what I constantly preach to everyone. The moment I was in a position where I had to trust God and have faith, it put so much into perspective. Giving godly advice always sounds great until you have to apply it to your own life. It's easy to have faith when the bills are paid, everyone is healthy, and you are having a good week at your job. But faith isn't really activated until it's tested.

You have to exercise or activate your faith when you can't see the outcome. That is true and genuine faith because it puts you in a position to wholeheartedly trust God.

During those difficult times, you have a decision to make. You are either going to trust God or you aren't. When I was going through my challenges, no one around me could have faith for me. It was personal. It was something that could only be done for me and by me. During this period of time God was proving Himself to me. When I walked into Redner's grocery store in Camden, Delaware, on July 21, 2019, I never would have guessed I would be leaving by ambulance.

In life, anything can change without a moment's notice because nothing is truly constant in life but change. In life, those times are a hard pill to swallow, especially when you don't totally or wholeheartedly trust God. Life will never make any real sense until you decide you are going to live for God in spite of whatever may happen in your life.

There are two things that are hard for a Believer to accept, but once they do, their entire perspective on life changes. The first one is hard to accept as a Believer but is a game changer once accepted: *the life we are living right this moment is temporary*. Whether you believe in God or not, one thing is for certain: when you are born, you are destined to die! This is why, as a Believer, you have to live life with purpose. You have to live a life that's intentional. We are not going to be here forever, so we have to stop living life like we will be. We are on assignment. God has assignments for all of us as

Believers to complete for specific purposes. Every morning when I open my eyes, I thank God for opening my eyes because it indicates that He still has work for me to do. I ask God to lead me and guide me in everything, from what I say and do to where I go. We have to stop wasting our precious time with people God never intended for us to meet and in places God never intended us to go. I can't imagine dying and finally meeting God only for Him to say to me, "Out of all the things you did, all your good deeds and works had nothing to do with your assignment or the purpose I created you for. Your works never brought you into relationship with Me or gave Me any glory. I never knew you." I ask God to keep me in a place where I can hear His voice and am able to remain obedient to His word and will for my life.

The second is that our life is not our own. I can recall one of the devotions I read that resonated in my spirit more recently. The devotion stated, "We are stewards, not owners, of the life God has given us." I remember looking up the word "steward" on Merriam-Webster.com even though I already knew what it meant. I wanted to get even more clarity of such a powerful statement. Basically, a "steward" is someone who manages the property of someone else (Merriam-Webster .com, s.v. "steward," accessed June 30, 2021, https://www .merriam-webster.com/dictionary/steward). This life we are living is the gift God has given us, and we are called to be stewards of it. We are responsible for what happens with it while we are employing the body. We are on what my mom used to call "borrowed time." That means we need not waste the time God has given (gifted) us. Instead, we need to make good use of that time by completing what God has assigned us to do. We are to use the time to get our assignment done and fulfill our purpose.

Too often we do with our life what we want to do. As a Believer, that's the wrong thinking. We need to stop being so concerned with our own self-will and instead ask God what His will is for our lives. See, we can only truly fulfil purpose when we are doing God's will for our life. It's not purpose when we are solely doing our will for our life. I'm simply a servant of God. I listen for His voice and try to be obedient to what He wants me to do. It only makes sense to consult with the Creator who has created the assignment and, ultimately, the purpose for our life.

Ask God what He wants you to do right now in your life. God knows best. One of my favorite books in the Bible, for so many reasons, is Jonah. The main reason is that when God calls you to do an assignment, it's usually something that is uncomfortable. It's uncomfortable because the flesh naturally counters or goes against everything spiritual. That's why almost every assignment that truly comes from God is a struggle for your flesh or your mentality. Even if it's a struggle, the worst thing you can do when God has assigned you to a task is run and hide from the assignment. I wholeheartedly believe that that was the path I was taking right before I had my stroke. I was pulling away from my assignment. I was pulling away from my purpose. I was pulling away from God. The problem with that is that, at the end of the day, God's will will be done, whether you decide to be the one who carries it out or not.

Most of the time, we aren't concerned with what God wants us to do. We are too busy chasing the superficial things in life. We are chasing the things that will not mean anything once we take our last breath. Unfortunately, most times we measure life's value by our material possessions and/or our accomplishments and accolades. I would be lying if I said being financially stable doesn't help, having the luxuries of life doesn't help, or having credit doesn't help because they absolutely do help in this life. All of those *things* help alleviate some of the burdens of life. Yet none of those things can equate to having God. Therefore, don't chase money, power, position, or prestige in life. Chase purpose!

This doesn't mean don't look for promotions that bring you more money or elevate you so you become financially stable. This doesn't mean don't work to establish yourself to have vehicles and houses. This doesn't mean don't do what's right to get or maintain good credit. It simply means keep what's important a priority. My daily petition to God is that He will keep me in a place where I can hear His voice. I remain obedient to His word and will for my life. Don't let the things of this world, from material things to accomplishments and accolades, ever cloud your spiritual sight. I don't care how good it looks to this world, we as Believers are in this world, but not of (or a part of) this world.

Today I look at life very differently. What should stand out the most about life is what you discover or learn on your journey through it. Life should always teach you something, whether you learn from something good or you learn from something bad. I have gained more insight from life through God. Even as I wrote this book, I observed that God's hand was on my life long before I even realized it—long before I got married, long before my daughter verbally committed for college, and long before I had my strokes. What was so obvious before any of those events, and even more so after everything I have experienced, is that life is valuable.

Every day is now even more like a holiday for me. Not to sound profound, but when you have honestly experienced a traumatic incident but have managed to find the blessing in it (not the blessing of going through the trauma, but the blessing in making it through, or surviving, the trauma), you recognize that every day is a blessing. Every day affords you another opportunity to reflect, repent, and then get it right. Your reflection should give you the ability to see how far God has brought you in both the natural and spiritual aspects of your life. If you are still here after the past year or more of challenges from a pandemic, race wars, and the war in politics, it should be even more obvious that you have purpose. That's not to say that those who didn't make it didn't have purpose. But the reality of it is that you are still here to get the assignment done, so do just that. Get it done.

The past two years have been quite a journey. From having

two strokes, to watching my baby girl commit to a Division 1 college, to marrying my best friend, I have experienced both highs and lows, and I wouldn't have been able to go through it, understand it, or endure any of it without God. There is still more I could say, but there are really no words to fully describe this journey of my life experiences except for God. Is. Faithful.

Every day God allows us to open our eyes is a gift. We must learn how to truly cherish and appreciate every moment because we honestly don't know when it will be our last. Grateful doesn't even begin to scratch the surface of how appreciative I am to God that He let me live; I am still here, with no residue from the strokes, sane and healthy. That's no testament of how great I am. It is a true testament of who God is. What I am coming to appreciate, more and more, is that my purpose on this earth is much bigger than "Tiffany."

I am humbled that God chose me for such a time as this. I am grateful for the good, the bad, and the ugly that has taken place in my life. Today I am grateful for my amazing husband, my loving and supportive family, my wonderful daughter, the friends I consider family, and the students (past and present) He has allowed in my life. Today I am grateful for a purpose-driven life. I will continue to stay the course, despite what life has in store for me. My daily mantra will forever be "God, if you lead, I will follow." I can't think of a better path to be on but the one that leads to God.

YOU CAN CONTINUE TO
FOLLOW ME ON MY JOURNEY AT
ToughTalkWithTiffany.com

Made in the USA
Middletown, DE
12 December 2021

53768551R00092